ONCE PART OF ILLYRIA,
WHICH NOW BOSNIA IS CALLED,

A WILD LAND,
BUT RICH IN SILVER ORE.

THERE ARE NO WIDE PLAINS
AMONG THE RIDGES HERE,

NOR FIELDS TO GIVE
THE GREATEST HARVEST,

BUT THE SAVAGE MOUNTAINS,
BARE, HIGH ROCKS

AND THE TALL TOWERS
STANDING ON THE SHEER CREST.

IOANNES PANNONIUS
(1434–1472)

Publisher	Vrijeme, Zenica
Author	Emir Suljagić
Editor	Muamer Spahić
Translation	Nina Begović
Design and Layout	Kenan Zekić
DTP	Fatima Zimić
Photos	Amel Emrić
	(pp. 37, 40, 47, 64, 69, 80, 91)
	Danilo Krstanović
	(pp. 11, 21, 22, 25, 71, 75, 85, 89, 92, 104, 109, 111)
	Philipp von Recklinghausen
	(pp. 32, 34, 42, 45, 48, 52, 72, 118)
	Dado Ruvić
	(pp. 12, 18, 62, 107, 127, 130)
Print	Suton, Široki Brijeg
ISBN	978-9958-18-085-9

Zenica, 2017

SREBRENICA
MCMXCV

CONTENTS

THE GENOCIDE

THE GUILT

REMEMBRANCE

THE DIRECTORY 133

CHRONOLOGY 149

INTRODUCTION

The Genocide Operation

In July 1995, the military and police forces of the Republika Srpska killed over 8,000 Bosnian Muslim men in Srebrenica in just a few days. In parallel to the execution of males of all ages, the political and military leadership of the Republika Srpska ordered the forced displacement of women and children from the enclave of Srebrenica, which ended the process of ethnic cleansing in Podrinje, initiated in April 1992. Prior to these executions and forced displacement, the authorities of the Republika Srpska had enforced enclave living conditions on the population of the Srebrenica region that would have ultimately lead to their partial or total destruction. Several years of torture, persecution, as well as the final mass execution, took place in an area declared a UN "safe area" by the United Nations Security Council, in Resolution 819. Consequently, the International Court of Justice in The Hague – The ICJ – and the International Criminal Tribunal for the former Yugoslavia – The ICTY – have both ruled that the crimes in Srebrenica were acts of genocide.

The genocide operation which started after the fall of Srebrenica on 11th July 1995 and ended five days later, was the most demanding operation undertaken by military and civil authorities of Bosnian Serbs supported by the Republic of Serbia during the aggression against Bosnia and Herzegovina. All political and military activities were directed to this same aim – the extermination of the Bosnian population in the Srebrenica enclave.

Such a comprehensive operation required the participation of the entire society. Even more than its scale, this crime is particularly terrifying because of the intimate relations that previously existed between the executioners and their victims. The victims were transported to their deaths by the very buses that used to drive them to work, and they were detained in their former classrooms. Although some executions were carried out by military or police units whose members were not from Eastern Bosnia, the majority of victims were killed by former friends, neighbours, colleagues and schoolmates.

The decision to only exterminate the male population instead of killing entire families in the Srebrenica enclave was taken to avoid the political consequences of an indictment for genocide. However, ultimately the result was the same at a societal level, since the men in the rather traditional patriarchal Muslim community of Eastern Bosnia had a leading role in public as well as in private life. The men were more educated, they were the bread-winners, the protectors, and the decision makers in their families. Execution of the male members of the community, at the same time as forced displacement of women, children, and the elderly, had identical consequences: the total destruction of the pre-war structure and community of Bosnian Muslims in Eastern Bosnia.

Today the ethnic group we knew as Bosnian Muslims or Bosniaks is a disempowered minority in this part of the country.

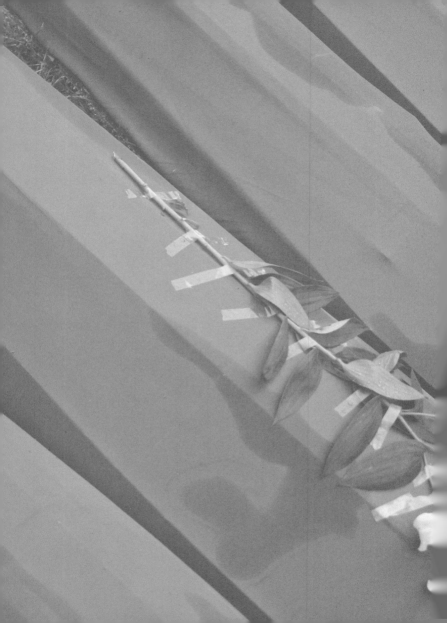

DISSOLUTION

Srebrenica – A Short History

Srebrenica is a town located in the north-east of Bosnia, which borders on the munici-palities of Bratunac, Vlasenica, Han-Pijesak, Rogatica, and Višegrad. The history of the town of Srebrenica goes back to Roman times, when the Srebrenica settlements of Gra-dina, Skelani, and Klotjevac were mentioned as important places, traversed by Roman roads. Since the Romans ex-cavated ores in Srebrenica, mostly silver, the nearby min-ing city of Domavium became a thriving colony. The devel-opmental peak of this Roman settlement was recorded in the third century, when its popula-tion reached nearly 30,000 people, making Domavium one of the larger European settlements.

The first mention of Srebrenica in medieval Bosnia was in 1352, but it was to reach the height of its development at the beginning of 15th century, when it achieved the status of a town, with its own currency mint. The Republic of Ragusa (present-day Dubrovnik) had a trading colony within the neighbourhood of Srebrenica, which precipitated the arrival of the first Franciscans to the town. This is why the Francis-can province is still called *Silver Bosnia*.

With the fall of the medieval Bosnian state and the estab-lishment of Ottoman authori-ties, Srebrenica remained an important centre of trade. The famous Ottoman travel writer Evliya Celebi recorded that the city of that period had 800

Srebrenica (*The Silver City*)

houses, six mosques, and 70 shops selling local handicrafts.

During the 1860s, the dissolution of the Ottoman Empire in the Balkans led to the mass migration of the Muslim population from Serbia, particularly from its western borders, to Eastern Bosnia, including the area of Srebrenica. Prior to this, and following the loss of the Ottoman territories in Europe, the town was inhabited by a significant Muslim population forcedly displaced from Hungary, who preserved their Hungarian family names and other particularities until their extinction in the genocide in 1995.

During the First and Second World Wars, Srebrenica suffered a high level of destruction and the Muslim and Serb populations endured considerable atrocities. After the Second World War, Srebrenica saw a boom in development and quickly became the centre of economic growth of the entire region. A factory producing car batteries, and a processing plant for metal products were built in Potočari, the town's industrial zone. Throughout the former state of Yugoslavia, the town also became renowned for its thermal spa, Guber, which was a thriving centre for health tourism.

The cultural life of the town concentrated around the Cultural Centre, which housed two cinema halls, a museum collection, a library, a folk dancing group, a theatre hall, and other facilities. There were eight primary schools in the municipality, as well as one of the best equipped high school in Bosnia and Herzegovina.

According to the last pre-war official census, the municipality of Srebrenica had a population of 36,666 in 81 settlements. Out of that total number, 27,572 (75,19%) were Bosniaks, 8,315 (22,67%) Serbs, 38 (0,10%) Croats, and 380 people (1,03%) who declared themselves as Yugoslavians. In summary, by 1991 the population of Srebrenica

Radovan Karadžić in the Parliament of B&H

made their living by working in factories in the Potočari industrial zone, the Sase mine, the wood processing industry in Zeleni Jadar, the metal packaging manufacturing plant in Skelani, as well as in agriculture, which provided work for one fourth of the employed population.

The Dissolution of Yugoslavia

In the summer of 1991, the Council of Ministers of the European Economic Community was trying to peacefully resolve the crisis in Yugoslavia and had established an Arbitrary Commission. The Commission (also known as Badinter's Arbitrary Committee after its chairman, the then President of the Constitutional Court of France, Robert Badinter), proposed that the so-called Brussels Declaration on Yugoslavia be adopted. It confirmed the dissolution of the Socialist Federal Republic of Yugoslavia (SFRY), and called upon its constituent republics to decide on independence, promising their international recognition by January 1992.

Due to the ethnic specificities, the Commission recommended that a referendum on independence should be organised in Bosnia and Herzegovina. In October 1991, Radovan Karadžić, President of the Serb Democratic Party (SDS*) publically threatened Bosnian Muslims with extermination should they insist on independence:

"Don't think that you won't lead Bosnia and Herzegovina into hell, and possibly the Muslim people into extermination", (Karadžić speaking in the Parliament of Bosnia and Herzegovina).

Four days prior to the deadline set by the international community for Bosnia and Herzegovina to decide on independence, the self-established Assembly of the Serb People decided, illegally and contrary

---

* SDS – Serb Democratic Party (*Srpska demokratska stranka* in Bosnian). (Explanation by the translator.)

to the Constitution, to establish the so-called Serb Republic of Bosnia and Herzegovina, which was officially proclaimed on 9th January 1992.

Independence of B&H

The Parliament of Bosnia and Herzegovina officially announced the referendum on independence of the country at its session on 25th January 1992. The referendum was held on 29th February and 1st March.

The SDS activists recommended that Serbs boycott the referendum. Despite this, over two thirds of the total electoral body voted in favour of sovereignty and independence, which according to international legal standards and the decision of the Badinter's Committee, was more than adequate to ensure international recognition of the state, which followed shortly after.

On 12th May 1992, the illegal Assembly of the Serb Republic of Bosnia and Herzegovina (later renamed 'Republika Srpska') adopted the 'Strategic Goals of the Serb People in Bosnia and Herzegovina'. One of the most important goals (Number 3) concerned the area of Eastern Bosnia:

"Establishment of a corridor in the valley of the Drina River, meaning the elimination of the Drina River border between the two Serb states", which clearly showed the intention to eliminate the Bosniak people in Eastern Bosnia. Ratko Mladić was duly appointed as Commander of the Army of the Republika Srpska and the genocide operation begun. At this session, Mladić himself clearly stated that the political goals of the Serb Republic of Bosnia and Herzegovina could not be realized without genocide.

Sometime later, in January 1994, speaking about the Bosniaks at this same Assembly he stated: "The only thing I am interested in is for them to completely disappear".

lista »Oslobođenje«
"ODUVIJEK SE LJUDI OVDJE
DIJELE ISKLJUČIVO NA
RAJU I PAPKE"
mbo
RAJA SU
ZA
EDJELJIVU I
NEZAVISNU
BOSNU
A PAPCI ...

Arming the Serb Population

In the summer of 1989, the State Security Service of the Ministry of Interior of Serbia prepared a document labelled "state secret, highly confidential", which had the aim of spreading a wave of "anti-bureaucracy revolution" in former Yugoslavia. This initiative led directly to Slobodan Milošević rising to power in Serbia, Kosovo, Vojvodina, and Montenegro, and later in Bosnia and Herzegovina.

This report, entitled "Reasons for Emigration of Serbs from Central Podrinje and the Municipalities of Srebrenica and Bratunac" – was unprecedented in former Yugoslavia and seriously disturbed relations between the two republics, especially after Borisav Jović, SFRY (Socialist Federal Republic of Yugoslavia) Presidency member from Serbia and one of Milošević's subordinates, put it on the agenda of the SFRY Presidency session. The document became public be-

cause the presidency member for Bosnia and Herzegovina, Bogić Bogićević, informed the authorities, and later representatives of the media, about its existence. Apart from the fact that this report by the Serbian State Security was factually incorrect, the serious scandal was caused by the fact that the Serbian State Security agents were active in the territory of Bosnia and Herzegovina in secrecy, contrary to the law, and without the authority to do so.

Although the report's initial aim was not realised, it nevertheless widened the ethnic divisions among the local population. The establishment of ethnic political parties and the first multiparty elections in 1990, as well as the clear ambitions of the Serb Democratic Party to divide everything – from authority and state institutions to trade unions, schools and state-owned companies – have since determined the substance and dynamics of relations between

Genocide Announcement

According to the ruling by the International Criminal Tribunal for the former Yugoslavia (ICTY), the "Decision on the Strategic Goals of the Serb People in Bosnia and Herzegovina" was a precursor of the genocide committed in Srebrenica. Radovan Karadžić elaborated the war goals of the Serb People to delegates of so-called Assembly of the Serb Republic of Bosnia and Herzegovina:

"It seems that there is no need for us to agree on any of the goals. The goal has been imprinted deeply within us. It is sacred because it is divine and because it was not put there by human hand. This is the goal the Serb people have long been nurturing, the goal never to be given up on, no matter how hard the times. We had to agree on tactics, make arrangements for practical solutions, but we didn't have to discuss the far-reaching strategic goals because we all had one same thought in our minds. And this is the safest guarantee that it comes from the deepest being of the Serb people; from deep inside of each of its members.

There are ethnic communities unable to live together in the heart of Europe. This is simply because they hinder each other's development. There are species among plants that cannot grow together. They have to be separated in order to grow."

the Serbs and the more numerous Bosniak population in Eastern Bosnia.

Following the establishment of the SAO (Serb Autonomous Area) Birač – which actually was a parallel authority in this area – there was no doubt that the aim of the SDS was to establish an exclusively Serb state within the borders of Bosnia and Herzegovina. Organised by the SDS and the Yugoslav National Army (YNA), the arming of the Serb population in Bosnia and Herzegovina began.

THE SIEGE

Tightening of the Noose

In April 1992, units of the YNA (Yugoslav National Army) Novi Sad Corps and Serb paramilitary forces took over the city of Srebrenica without encountering resistance. At this stage, only a few hundred of its pre-war citizens remained in the town. Srebrenica remained under the control of Serb authorities for one month, a period marked by plunder and crime.

By the end of April 1992, a group of self-organised volunteers from Srebrenica initiated the first conflict with the soldiers from the YNA, paramilitary forces, and the local Serb police. A month later, in the village of Bajramovići all independent armed groups held a meeting and established the Headquarters of the Srebrenica Territorial Defence Forces.

Naser Orić was named commander. Serb forces withdraw from Srebrenica on 19th May 1992, pressured by the Territorial Defence Forces of Bosnia and Herzegovina.

Torture in Phases

The siege of Srebrenica can be divided into two periods. The first one lasted from May 1992 until April 1993. During this period, Srebrenica became a refuge for the Bosniak population that survived the first wave of violence along the Drina valley. From the beginning of the siege, the Serb forces regularly attacked the enclave, so that its borders were not stable and were changing constantly. By the summer of 1992, hunger had already become the

central concern of each citizen of the enclave. By the end of this period, in April 1993, the so-called "safe area" of Srebrenica was established.

The second period lasted from April 1993 until July 1995, when the enclave was nominally under the protection of the UN. The establishment of the UN "safe area" of Srebrenica put no end to the torment of the enclave's inhabitants, which included the domestic population along with those internally displaced from the villages of the Srebrenica Municipality, whose homes had been taken over by Serb forces, and refugees from other parts of Eastern Bosnia who had left their villages during the previous year due to the occupation by Serb forces.

Life in Hell

During the first several months after liberation, Srebrenica functioned without any political authorities. It was only at the beginning of July 1992 that the War Presidency of Srebrenica was established. Thus the inhabitants lost any form of organisation, and the only law was the threat of violence.

Nevertheless, the territory under the control of units of the Army of the Republic of Bosnia and Herzegovina in Eastern Bosnia during the summer of 1992, had grown and extended towards the north, in the direction of Tuzla. During the months to follow, the fighting was to become more intense, and by autumn there was fighting for control of the areas along the road Bratunac – Konjević-Polje.

As a result of the direct interference of Serbia and the Yugoslav Army, the persecution of the non-Serb population continued. By spring 1993, as a result of the persecution in other settlements in Eastern Bosnia, the population of Srebrenica increased significantly and reached between 50,000 and 60,000 people.

Hunger Changes People

After the pre-war food reserves came to an end, people started eating rye and oats. It was not possible to sift or process flour made from these seeds, so the result was bitter and difficult to swallow. For some citizens of the enclave, the constant feeling of hunger was worse than the fear of shells and sniper bullets. Hunger changes people terribly, and sometimes people did unthinkable things to each other out of hunger; ready to even risk their lives for one piece of yellow cornbread.

For people who lived in the countryside, the issue of hunger was easier to cope with since they owned land which could be cultivated, however, with the land in this area barely arable, their crops were barely enough to feed their families. Two small convoys of humanitarian aid arrived in December 1992, but were not enough to ease the hunger.

Money soon became worthless and an alternative market evolved where goods were exchanged with goods. The value of the most important items for trade was dictated by the war i.e. by the relation between the armed forces on the battlefield. Only cigarettes could still be bought with money. By the end of winter 1992, cigarettes became scarce goods, reaching the unbelievable price of 75 to 100 Euros a packet.

When in March 1993 Serb forces started encroaching on the town, people from the surrounding villages started arriving in Srebrenica with bundles quickly packed into horse carts and on livestock. The livestock they brought along were soon slaughtered, so during those first days it was possible to exchange a kilo of meat for a kilo of corn at the town market. But by the next week it was possible to get several kilos of meat for a kilo of corn.

Food from the Sky

By the beginning of 1993, when it became clear that the authorities of the Republika Srpska were not going to allow any convoys into Srebrenica, the then president of the USA, Bill Clinton, decided to airdrop food to the enclaves in Eastern Bosnia. American planes started dropping pallets and packages of food, and thousands of people took to the hills, with or without torches, some in groups some alone, led only by their instincts. Searching for food soon became a lottery in which you risked your life.

By April 1993, when the UN Commander Phillipe Morillon arrived in Srebrenica, people were eating anything they could find: corncobs, hazel bushes, anything that seemed remotely digestible. During the entire summer and autumn, hundreds of civilians would cross Serb positions around the enclave at night, walk kilometres into the territory under Serb control to the torched and destroyed Muslim villages in search for food remains, and then return before dawn. It was a race against death, darkness, ambushes and unthinkable physical exertion. No one will ever find out how many people fell victim to the "food search".

Unbearable Suffering

On top of this terrible issue of hunger, another deprivation was the severe shortage of salt. It was possible to buy almost anything on the black market, except for salt. Those who had it until the spring of 1993 did not want to sell it on. Sometime in the middle of winter that year, someone discovered the reserves of road salt, which would yield a tiny snow-white film of salt after hours of cooking.

Only the calamity of being wounded was perhaps worse than death in the besieged town of Srebrenica.

Operation "Parachute"

"With the first sound of the plane engine the entire town springs to their feet and the remaining inhabitants immediately run to the hilltops. For a moment everybody falls silent and listens to see if they are going to drop over the city or continue towards Žepa. With the sound of a clattering parachute, hundreds of people race towards the place of impact in a stampede. They have nothing to light their way, but within minutes they are already in the woods, looking for parcels. They cross the stream despite the snow, climb up the back of the hillsides and down into narrow ravines, calling to each other and asking where the parcels have dropped. Only shadows are visible in the dark, panting with strain, running through the woods to get to the food before others find it. Old women and men jostle. People swear at each other. And when, after a few minutes, the parcel is finally spotted, dozens of hands pounce upon it, ripping the cardboard and snatching as much as possible. People elbow one another; there are shots; knives are drawn. Two women fight over a meal. An old lady loses consciousness after failing to find anything for herself, and mentions her children in her delirium. A man is eating the leftovers from a can which had burst in its fall, and another is asking him to spare some food for him.

Each box is gets checked a dozen times. An hour after the airdrop, the hunt in the woods is still on, and cardboard is set on fire to help locate for cans that have fallen off of the pallets. When the food has all been taken away, the parachute is ripped to pieces with a knife to be used for tailoring clothes. (...) The next morning, the place of the airdrop can be recognised by the rubble and the packaging of eaten meals; there is no one around and it is peaceful. Until the next night."

Haris Nezirović, journalist of the B&H weekly magazine "Slobodna Bosna"
(After having entered besieged Srebrenica at the beginning
of April 1993 and spent almost a month there.)

The majority of surgical procedures were performed without anaesthetics, and desperate patients would offer all they owned in exchange for medicines. Often the cost was more than they owned.

Slow-motion Genocide

Contact with the outside world was possible only thanks to Ham radio. Their first job was to publish lists of people exiled from Podrinje to the city of Tuzla, and other places in North Eastern Bosnia, and who had therefore survived attacks or had been deported. Every day hundreds of people continued the search for their family members and friends, browsing through those lists displayed at the entrance of the post office. The only way to get in touch with family members was through the amateur radio operators.

On 18th March 1993, Sadako Ogata, UN High Commissioner for Refugees, sent a dramatic report on the situation in the Srebrenica enclave to the UN Secretary General Boutros Ghali:

"Thousands of people are entering the town from surrounding areas that have been systematically attacked and occupied by the Serb forces. Thirty to forty people have already died of hunger or because of a shortage of medical help. There is every indication that the enclave of Srebrenica is witnessing a mass humanitarian tragedy."

At that time, Lieutenant General Philippe Morillon, UNPROFOR Commander in Bosnia and Herzegovina, arrived in Srebrenica from the village of Konjević-Polje, which had been seized by Serb forces. When Morillon was stopped from an attempt to secretly leave the enclave, he spoke to the panicking Srebrenica citizens from a military transporter, declaring that the town was under the protection of the UN. Reacting to the "rapid

Everything Smelled of Death

"While passing by the town hospital I often heard screaming that made my blood run cold. I would start walking faster to get away as soon as possible, but the screams could be heard even at a distance from the building. Limbs were amputated without anaesthetics or the use of any medical surgical instruments. Hand saws were often used, with the flesh cut by the blade, and the bone by the saw. Sometimes, relatives would bring a litre of brandy in order for the wounded person to get drunk before the amputation. But this could be dangerous, since it could cause massive bleeding and carried the risk of bleeding to death. There were clotheslines around the hospital where reused bandages were hung to dry, and the entire building was surrounded with this wall of dirty-yellow bandages. Inside, everything smelled of pus, turning the stomachs of those who weren't used to the stench. It was pus as well as sweat that stank badly, as well as human faeces. Everything in this hospital and around it reeked. Dead bodies were rank, for sometimes there would be dozens of them piled up in the morgue. Everything smelled of death.

Somehow deep inside, I was convinced that I would never find myself a patient in this hospital. I imagined that I would only be brought there if I were dead. I was not afraid of death, but like everyone else I feared the possibility of a leg or hand amputation with the saw. Whenever a grenade would whistle overhead, whenever an explosion was heard, while waiting for it to fall, I prayed to God for

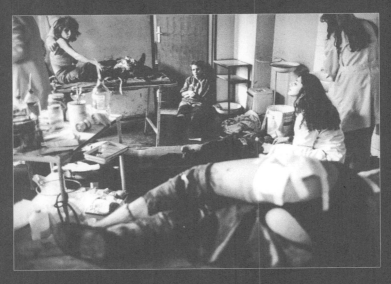

a bullet or a grenade to kill me instantly. To save me from
the suffering. And I was confident that everyone else did
the same. We all thought that we were already dead, just
waiting for that final moment, that day when death would
come to get us, and we were all terrified by the thought
that a grenade could cripple us. This was the thing we
feared the most. And death? Well, it was our friend. Our
travel-mate. It never left us. It was always there, together
with the hunger. These two friends were always with us."

Hasan Nuhanović, The Escape (Srebrenica, autumn 1992)

deterioration of the situation in Srebrenica and its surroundings", on 16th April 1993 the UN Security Council adopted Resolution 819, which formally declared Srebrenica a UN "safe area".

Based on this Security Council Resolution, the UNPROFOR forces mediated the Ceasefire Agreement between the RB&H (Republic of Bosnia and Herzegovina) Army and the RS Army, which was signed on 18th April 1993. Upon the UN's insistence, and although this was not part of the Resolution, a clause on the demilitarisation of the RB&H Army forces in Srebrenica was included in the Ceasefire Agreement. On the same day, the first UNPROFOR members arrived in Srebrenica, a unit from a Canadian Battalion who were part of the UN forces in Bosnia and Herzegovina.

However, despite the fact that Srebrenica had been proclaimed a UN safe area, the humanitarian situation remained desperate. During his visit to the Security Council mission in April 1993, Ambassador Diego Arria, Permanent Representative of Venezuela to the UN Security Council, described the situation in Srebrenica as a "slow-motion genocide under the protection of the UN forces".

A Brief Feeling of Security

Following the deployment of the UN forces in the enclave, it seemed as if the war's intensity was decreasing. However, hygienic conditions were still critical – lice and scab infestations appeared. In search for food at that time, people even resorted to rummaging through the Dutch Battalion's garbage dump.

Summer and fall of 1993 passed by in bland euphoria due to the sense of security established for the first time since the beginning of the war. Convoys with humanitarian aid started arriving and briefly put

an end to the fear of hunger. However, though there were no major attacks during that period, snipers positioned on higher ground continued shooting at the town. Momir Nikolić, Security Officer of the RS Army Bratunac Brigade, defined this situation as "... making life in the enclave difficult, preventing civilians from doing their jobs".

At this time, some people took the great risk of leaving the enclave to go towards Tuzla in smaller or larger groups. Others crossed over to Serbia via Žepa, and then to Macedonia. The authorities were powerless in preventing them to leave. Two years later, there was no longer a cohesive community in the enclave; it was simply a crowd of individuals, without any kind of organised mutual support, facing an uncertain future.

During this period, UNHCR evacuated between eight and nine thousand people from Srebrenica, against the ob-jection of the Government of RB&H, which considered that such actions meant that the United Nations were participating in ethnic cleansing.

In March 1994, the Canadian Battalion handed over their duties to a Dutch Battalion in the "safe area" of Srebrenica.

Directive by Karadžić

By the end of July 1994, the RS Army General Staff informed the corps commanders that the Ceasefire Agreement from 18 April 1993 "was suspended". The Drina Corps received orders to reduce the enclave of Srebrenica to the territory of the town only, and the enclave of Žepa to a territory of three kilometres.

By spring of 1995, the RS authorities started to believe that the war had to be brought to an end soon. In March, RS president Karadžić issued the Directive 7 of the Supreme Command. Karadžić's strategy was simple: to forcedly end

"Podrinje must be Serbian Territory"

Lieutenant Colonel Slavko Ognjenović, Commander of the Bratunac Brigade which controlled a part of the encirclement around Srebrenica, wrote in a document dated 4th July 1994:

"We have won the war in Podrinje, but didn't finish off the Muslims, which has to be done during the period to come. We have to realise the final goal – to make Podrinje entirely Serb. The enclaves of Srebrenica, Žepa, and Goražde have to be militarily defeated. We must continuously equip, train, drill and prepare the RS Army to execute this crucial task – the expulsion of Muslims from the Srebrenica enclave. There must be no retreat around the enclave, we must only move forward. We have to make our enemy's life miserable, thus making life in the enclave unbearable in order for them to realise that survival in the enclave is impossible."

the war and coerce the international community into accepting the factual state in the field. The Drina Corps was to implement this strategy.

At this time, the Srebrenica defence Commander Naser Orić and fifteen younger officers of the 28th Division of the RB&H Army left Srebrenica by order of the Supreme Command in Sarajevo, to attend training. By the beginning of May, a part of this group tried to return but their helicopter was shot down near Žepa; twelve people died and ten were wounded.

Tightening the Noose

A full-scale rehearsal of the attack was organised in June, in order to test the will and capacity of the international community to protect the "safe zones". Upon the orders of the Drina Corps Commander Milenko Živanović, on 3rd June 1995, units from the Bratunac Brigade and the special military unit "Wolves

of the Drina" took control of the UN observation post in the village of Zeleni Jadar. The battle report of the Drina Corps, which was sent to the headquarters on the same day states: "the population of Zeleni Jadar [...] fled in panic", and "it was observed that the people from the wider territory of Zeleni Jadar moved towards Srebrenica after UNPROFOR's retreat". As a result of this attack, the population of the actual town increased from 36,000 to 42,000. Around 85 per cent of them were refugees. The noose had tightened.

Plan "Krivaja-95"

On Saint Vitus' Day (28th June) 1995, Radovan Karadžić and Momčilo Krajišnik, president of the Serb Assembly, visited the command of the Drina Corps in Vlasenica. General Krstić, Corps Chief of Staff, was also invited to the meeting. Karadžić asked Krstić

KOMANDA DRINSKOG KORPUSA   VOJNA TAJNA
Strogo pov.br. **04/156-2**   STROGO POVERIJIVO
02.07.1995.godine   PRIMERAK BR. **2**
                                             "KRIVAJA - 95"

                                                    00847289

        KOMANDI: 1.Zpbr, 1.Bpbr, 2.Rmtbr
                 1.Brlpbr, 1.Mlpbr, 5.map

        ZAPOVEST ZA AKTIVNA b/d Op.br.1

Sekcije: 1: 50.000 Zvornik 3 i 4 i Višegrad 1 i 2

1. - Neprijatelj je u sklopu opšte ofanzive na teritoriju RS
izvodio napade sa ograničenim ciljem prema jedinicama DK.
Cenimo da će neprijatelj u narednom periodu prema z/o DK inten-
zivirati ofanzivna dejstva sa težištem na Tuzlansko-Zvorničkom
i Kladanjsko-Vlaseničkom pravcu uz istovremeno dejstvo snaga
28.pd iz enklava Srebrenica i Žepa radi presecanja z/o DK i
spajanja enklava sa centralnim dijelom teritorije bivše BiH
koju drže muslimanske snage.
Poslednjih nekoliko dana posebno su aktivne muslimanske snage
iz enklava Žepa i Srebrenica.
Ubacuje DTG koje napadaju i pale nezaštićena sela, ubijaju civi-
lno stanovništvo i izdvojene manje jedinice oko enklava Žepa i
Srebrenica. Posebno je uporan u spajanju enklava i stvaranju
koridora ka Kladnju.
Prema raspoloživim podacima snage 28.d su angažovane po sledećem:

- 288. brigada zatvara pravac s. Potočari - Srebrenica, u gotovosti je za aktivna dejstva ka Bratuncu i presecanje komunikacije
Bratunac - s. Glogova - Konjević Polje. KM u s. Budak.
Posebno je utvrdio i čvrsto će braniti objekte Zonik, industri-
jsku zonu u Potočarima, rejon s. Likar i Gradac /tt.527/.

- 281. brigada zatvara pravac s. Podgaj - Borovac /tt.730/ -
s. Sućeska, u gotovosti za ofanzivna dejstva ka s.Derventa i
s.Koprivno. KM u rejonu Sućeska. Posebno je čvrsto uredio i
krajnje uporno će braniti Borovac /tt.730/, s. Žedanjsko, s. Sуće-
ska i Kok /tt.946/.

- 282. brigada zatvara pravac Zeleni Jadar - Srebrenica, u gotovosti za napadna dejstva ka Skelzzica. . KM s.Bojna.
Posebno je utvrdio i krajnje uporno će braniti posumljene vi-
sove severno 300m od Zelenog Jadra, Prljuha, Živkovo br /tt.780/,
rejon s.Pusmulića, tt.664, rejon Bojna i Vagan /tt.843/.

- 283. brigada zatvara pravad Podravanje - s. Bučje - Vijogor, u
gotovosti za aktivna dejstva ka Podravanju i Rudniku Braćan.
Obezbedjenje koridor Srebrenica - Žepa.

The battle plan to attack Srebrenica – "Krivaja-95"

when the army could attack Srebrenica. Krstić answered that he needed three to five days. Karadžić told him to shorten the preparations and that he would get whatever he needed. After this meeting, the Drina Corps Command started preparing the battle plan to attack Srebrenica – "Krivaja-95".

On 2nd July 1995, the Drina Corps received orders "to go into offensive action with its free forces (...) in order to separate the enclaves of Žepa and Srebrenica and reduce them to the municipal area". In accordance with this order "the preconditions for elimination of the enclaves" needed to be created.

Two tactical groups were formed: one under the command of Vinko Pandurević, and the other commanded by Mirko Trivić. On 5th July, Pandurević and Trivić arrived in Zeleni Jadar. In the afternoon they received instructions and concrete orders for the attack.

"They should all be killed"

Two days before the beginning of the attack on Srebrenica, Radovan Karadžić invited Miroslav Deronjić, the most prominent SDS official in Podrinje, to come to Pale, the so-called capital of the new Republika Srpska. Following a short conversation about the possible consequences of taking military control over the enclave, Karadžić is reported as saying: "Miroslav, they should all be killed."

In his later testimony to the International Criminal Court for the former Yugoslavia during Slobodan Milošević's trial, Deronjić stated that Karadžić also specified:

"'Anything you find' using the pronoun *you* in plural. Then he added the following – 'West Slavonia principle'*. This is

---

* "West Slavonia" refers to the operation "Bljesak" undertaken by the Croatian Army in May 1995, after which the Serb population left this part of the country together with the army.

literally the sentence he used." During preparations for the attack, Serb forces prevented the delivery of humanitarian aid to Srebrenica, as well as a convoy with the supplies for the Dutch Battalion. At that time, the command of the Dutch Battalion was exclusively concerned with its own security and the state of its supplies, whereas the RB&H Army forces were panic-ridden. After two years of living under siege, the population of Srebrenica was lost and paralysed.

THE OFFENSIVE

Attack at 3 a.m.

At three o'clock in the morning, on 6th July 1995, the attack on Srebrenica began from all positions surrounding the city. Shelling was intensive and continuous. Five observation posts of the Dutch Battalion in the southern part of the enclave fell one after the other in the RS Army attack. The RB&H Army soldiers sought to prevent the withdrawal of the Dutch Battalion from the observation posts, but this attempt failed.

By the evening of 9th July, the RS Army had advanced four kilometres into the enclave, stopping only a kilometre from the centre of Srebrenica. Thus a line was established allowing complete control over the enclave borders and preventing any communication between Srebrenica and Žepa. The task was completed. However, on the same day, Karadžić issued an order authorising the RS Army to capture Srebrenica, thus changing the goal of the "Krivaja-95" operation. Reducing the enclave to the municipal area was no longer enough: the new order sought total seizure.

At dawn on 10th July, the 28th Division of the RB&H Army went into counterattack and almost succeeded in repulsing the attackers to their starting positions. However, this success was short-lived and by the evening of the same day the Serb forces had managed to recapture the lost positions. During the night of 10th July, the defenders started leaving the enclave. On the same day,

the RS Army headquarters decided to send additional forces to Srebrenica – the 10th Sabotage Unit and a newly formed police unit under the command of Ljubomir Borovčanin.

The Last Hope

That night the people from surrounding villages continued arriving in the town. Thousands of people, desperate for protection, crowded around the entrance of the pre-war company headquarters of Vezionica, which was located at the city entrance, and where one Dutch Battalion troop was still located.

Civilian and military authorities urged the UN to act in accordance with its mandate and protect Srebrenica. At a meeting, which lasted until late in the night, the Commander of the Dutch Battalion, Thom Karremans promised air strikes the next morning. But there were no air strikes and in the morning of 11th July, the Serb forces started taking over parts of the town. By four in the afternoon, Dutch soldiers had begun the operation to evacuate four to six thousand civilians from the town to Potočari. When the "Wolves of the Drina" and the 10th Sabotage Unit entered the city centre, it had been completely abandoned.

Gathering in Potočari

Women and men of all ages, as well as children, gathered in Potočari seeking refuge in the UN base. The real number of refugees who arrived there during 11th and 12th July shall never be determined. The Dutch Battalion estimated there were 17.500 people in Potočari, while the UN military observers considered the number was much higher – between 30.000 and 35.000.

On 11 July 1995, Serb forces took over the city. On the same day, Karadžić appointed Miroslav Deronjić as civilian commissioner for the "Serb

Srebrenica Municipality". In the early afternoon of 11th July, the Bosniak population of the enclave started arriving at the former battery factory in Potočari where the Dutch Battalion was located. People were advised to enter the factory area through a hole in the fence. Sometime around 18:00, the fence was closed. Between four and five thousand people sought refuge in the factory. The rest of the population settled in the neighbouring factories and garages of the nearby companies, and in empty houses.

It is evident today that during the 24 hours that followed, RS political and military authorities made two strategic decisions with tragic consequences: the first one – to deport the women and children from Potočari; the second – to kill the entire male population of the enclave.

Between 11th and 13th July, food and water were scarce in Potočari. People were exposed to unbearable heat during the day, while the nights were unusually cold. On 12th July, RS civilian authorities sent a fire fighting truck to Potočari, as well as several cistern trucks, some bread and candies that soldiers and RS Army officers gave out in front of TV cameras.

When the cameras went off, the soldiers took the food and water back. Fear spread through those gathered there; especially when some of the men were taken away and never seen again. Women were also singled out from the crowd; during the night, the darkness echoed with screaming, cries, gunfire...

Meeting in "Fontana"

At 8 p.m. on 11th July, a meeting was held between the representatives of the RS Army and the Dutch Battalion in Hotel Fontana in Bratunac. The RS Army delegation was led by general Mladić, followed by the intelligence and military security officers of the Drina Corps and the Supreme Command. Mladić ordered the Dutch Battalion Commander, Thom Karremans, to leave and return by 23:00 that same night with the representatives of the Muslim population located in Potočari. Karremans arrived at the second meeting together with Nesib Mandžić, a former teacher who had agreed to unofficially represent the Muslims gathered in Potočari.

After Mandžić explained that he did not have a mandate to negotiate on behalf of the military authorities or the entire population, Mladić asked to bring him the "people who can ensure surrender" by the following morning.

"All *Balija* should be killed"

Shortly before the third meeting in Hotel Fontana, during the morning of 12th July, Momir Nikolić met his senior colonel, Vujadin Popović, Assistant Chief for Security of the Drina Corps. Popović explained the plan to deport several thousand women and children from Potočari to territory under the control of the RB&H Army, near Kladanj, whereas the male population were to be separated, temporarily imprisoned in Bratunac, and later executed. According to his later testimony, Popović said: "All Balija* must be killed."

A day later, the plan changed and it was decided to transfer captured and imprisoned people from Srebrenica to the municipality of Zvornik and execute them there. This was decided after Miroslav Deronjić opposed any killings on the territory of Bratunac.

Around ten o'clock on 12th July, the third and last meeting took place in Hotel Fontana. This time, Mandžić and the Dutch Battalion officers were accom-

---

* 'Balija' is a derogatory term for descendants of Turks of the Ottoman Empire in the Balkans and for Bosnian ethnic and/or religious Muslims. (Explanation by the translator.)

panied by Ibro Nuhanović and Ćamila Omanović, although neither of them were officially representing military or civilian authorities of Srebrenica. Besides the officers, on this occasion Mladić's company consisted of representatives of civilian authorities from Bratunac. During the meeting, Mladić announced that the RS Army would provide vehicles for transporting people from the enclave towards the territory under RB&H Army control and that all males would undergo a "check". He ordered Dutch soldiers to escort the convoys. Bratunac Brigade Security Officer, Momir Nikolić, was in charge of "coordinating" the transportation of women and children and "separating out" men fit for military service.

"The Time of Revenge"

After entering Srebrenica, Ratko Mladić made a statement for the Serb Radio-Television (SRT):

"Here we are on 11th July, 1995 in the Serb Srebrenica. On the eve of another great Serb holiday, we would like to endow this city to the Serb people. Finally, after the popular uprising against the Turkish tyrants, the time has come to take revenge on the Turks on this territory."

This "Great Serb Holiday" was the Feast of Saints Peter and Paul (12th July), a liturgical feast in honour of apostles Saint Peter and Saint Paul, whereas the "rebellion against Turkish tyrants" in Serb history refers to the popular uprising against renegade Ottoman Janissary officers at the beginning of the 19th century on the same territory, which was then a Belgrade Province in central Serbia. Mladić's equalisation of Bosniaks and the Turks who ruled in the Balkans for five centuries is to be interpreted as the hatred, contempt, and low esteem in which Bosnian Muslims were held; a cultural prejudice which has been passed on through generations in Serb mythology, and as epic tales.

"Take them along the River Drina"

In the evening of 13th July 1995, an RS Army officer entered the office of Miroslav Deronjić in Bratunac, and introduced himself as Colonel Ljubiša Beara.

"He started talking and he said, I am not quoting his exact words, but he said something about him coming regarding the prisoners, that they should all be killed, if you understand (...) Since Beara explained the purpose of his visit, I told him that Karadžić had given me instructions that nothing should be done in Bratunac, and that detainees should be taken away towards Bijeljina, towards Batkovići, and also that I was not going to allow executions in Bratunac. He said that he had orders about what to do with the prisoners. He said: 'Mr. Deronjić, I have orders from the very top; the order from the top is to kill the prisoners.' And then he continued saying that all of them should be killed in Bratunac, and I answered that my instructions were that nothing was to be done there, but that they had to be taken away from Bratunac (...) He reluctantly agreed to what I was saying (...) This is where our conversation ended. It ended when I understood that I had convinced him that the detainees were to be taken along the river Drina to Zvornik or somewhere else. I didn't care where (...)."

Miroslav Deronjić, Statement by the witness,
Prosecutor vs. Slobodan Milošević,
http://www.icty.org/x/cases/slobodan_milosevic/
proswitness/bcs/mil-wit-deronjic.htm.

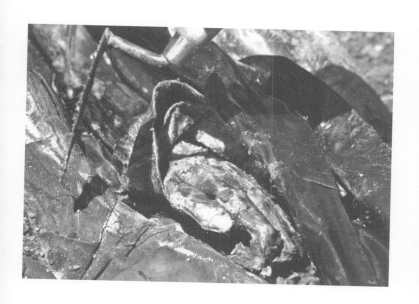

THE GENOCIDE

Mobilisation of Transport

Even before the negotiations in Hotel Fontana, Ratko Mladić had requested the Ministry of Defence of RS to send buses to the stadium in Bratunac by 14:30 the following day. In the early morning of 12th July, the Ministry ordered the urgent mobilisation of transport, and around 50 buses were sent from Pale, Sokolac, Rogatica, Višegrad, Han-Pijesak, Vlasenica, Milići, Bratunac, and Zvornik to the stadium in Bratunac. The municipal offices in Zvornik, Milići, Vlasenica, Šekovići, and Bratunac had the same orders. All regular bus lines were cancelled and all military transportation vehicles were made available for the deportation of the civil population from Potočari. The deportation required large amounts of fuel that at that time was chronically scarce. The Drina Corps sought permission from Headquarters to use 10,000 litres of diesel fuel and 2,000 litres of petrol to carry out the deportation.

The RS Ministry of Interior was also included in the process of deportation. In his report sent to superior officers on 13th July, Dragomir Vasić stated that the Ministry would be in charge of the "evacuation of the rest of the civil population from Srebrenica to Kladanj by buses (around 15.000)", and that this matter "urgently" required ten tons of oil. Buses started arriving in Potočari early in the afternoon on 12th July and police units started boarding civilians – women, children, and elderly men.

"The White House"

Men fit for military service were separated from the crowd, although among them were males younger than 15 and older than 65 years.

The men were taken into the so-called 'White House', a building located 150 metres from the main entrance to the Dutch Battalion base. The command of the Dutch Battalion received reports on maltreatment and the killing of men who were detained in the White House, and there were attempts to make lists of men located in front of the UN Battalion base, but the Dutch gave up such attempts after the threats they received. Any kind of access to the White House was forbidden to the UN.

The captured men were made to leave behind their personal belongings, ID cards, passports and other documents. On the evening of 13th July, all of them were transported from Potočari. The belongings they had left behind were burnt. Most of them were not seen alive ever again.

Murders in Bratunac

Men and boys separated from the mass in Potočari were taken to the "Vuk Karadžić" school and the old school in Bratunac. Miroslav Deronjić describes what Bratunac was like under siege that night:

"At that time many buses and trucks carrying imprisoned Muslims were arriving in Bratunac from Konjević-Polje. The buses were parked in the centre of town so everyone knew about it. People were taken away to the stadium, the hangar, and to the Vuk Karadžić High School. Many younger and older people were mobilised during the night. They were given guns and told to secure the buses. In the evening, Ljubo Simić reported on the murders and shootings that took place ..."

During that night, between eighty and one hundred people

republika srpska

02163049

ministarstvo unutrassnjih poslova
 kabinet ministra   very urgent ''ss''

broj: 64/95

datum: 10.07.1995. godine

-komandantu specijalne brigade policije
 -sstab komande policiskih snaga trnovo
 -sstab komande policiskih snaga vogosscca
 -sstab komande policiskih snaga bijeljina
 -cjb zvornik

-cjb sarajevo

-kamp za obuku policije jahorina

    na osnovu naredjenja vrhovnog komandanta oruzzanih snaga
republike srpske, a u cilju slamanja neprijateljske ofanzive
iz zassticene zone srebrenice:

                    n a r e d j u j e m

    1.izdvojiti dio snaga mup-a rs koji uchestvuje u borbenim
dejstvima na sarajevskom ratisstu i uputiti kao samostalnu
jedinicu u rajonu srebrenice u toku sutrassnjeg dana 11.07.1995.g.

    2. u sastav jedinice ulaze drugi specijalni odred policije
iz ssekovicca, prva cheta pjp cjb zvornik, mjessovita cheta
zdruzzenih snaga mup-a rsk-a, srbije i republike srpske i cheta
iz kampa centra za obuku na jahorini.

    3. za komandanta jedinice mup-a odredjujem ljubissu borov-
chanina zamjenika komandanta specijalne brigade policije.

    4. izvlachenje chete zdruzzenih snaga mup-a rsk-a, srbije i
republike srpske sa trnovskog ratisста izvrssiti u toku nocci.
okupljanje jedinice izvrssiti 11.07.1995. godine do 12 chasova
u bratuncu ispred sjb, osim drugog specijalnog ojreda policije
koji cce pokret ka odradisstu izvrssiti 11.07.1995. godine u
popodnevim satima.

    5.komandant jedinice je duzzan po dolasku na odredisste
stupiti u vezu sa nachelnikom sstaba korpusa generalom krsticcem.

komandant sstaba

tomislav kovach

The orders by the Ministry of Interior of the Republika Srpska
that clearly shows that the regular police forces of the Republic
of Serbia participated in operations in Srebrenica

"Don't shoot them in their heads – shoot them in the back"

"After the first bus was emptied, it was our turn (...) they took me to a lawn covered with corpses. A group of Serb soldiers were standing there. They stood in a line, shooting from automatic rifles and heavy machine-guns. I fell on the ground. My hands were tied behind my back so I fell on my face and stomach. A man fell over my head. I think he was killed instantly. I could feel his warm blood dropping on me. The shooting continued and then they ordered soldiers to shoot each one of us individually. I heard someone saying not to shoot peoples' heads because the brain explodes, but to shoot in the back. I was shot in the back. My hands were tied behind me, but the bullet went through under my left armpit just scratching me (...) they asked if anyone was wounded. Several people answered and were killed immediately."

(Testimony from a survivor of the execution at the Branjevo military farm. He testified as a protected witness under various codes. His last testimony was during Ratko Mladić's trial under the code RM-346.)

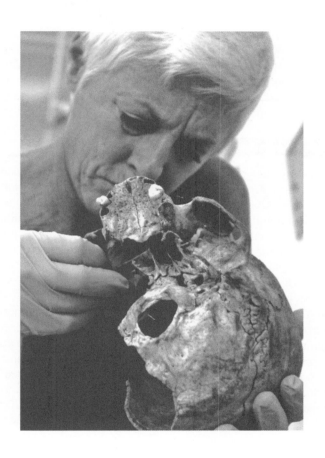

were killed in Bratunac. In the morning, a large number of detainees were transported towards Zvornik in a line of buses and trucks, which stretched to more than one and half kilometres. They were taken to several different locations and locked up in schools and sports halls.

Zvornik Brigade Scaffolds

The Military Intelligence Service of the RS Army played a central role in the organisation of the systematic killing of the male Bosniak population of the Srebrenica enclave. A group of officers from the Security Directorate, headed by Ljubiša Beara, planned the entire operation, the identification and mobilisation of resources, selection of human resources to perform the crimes and later the burying and destruction of evidence of the crimes. Members of the Military Police, as well as members of other units subordinate to the military security service also participated in the crimes.

The killings had already started in the evening of 11th July 1995, in Potočari, but the organised mass executions took place between 13th and 16th July in the municipalities of Bratunac and Zvornik. The five mass execution sites in Zvornik were: the school in Grbavci in the town of Orahovac, the dam near Petkovac, the Branjevo military farm, the Cultural Centre in Pilica, and the gravel pit in Kozluk. The largest site of mass execution in Bratunac was the warehouse of the Agricultural Cooperative in Kravica.

Organised Executions

The first large-scale execution took place in the afternoon of 13th July. The victims having been brought in buses and trucks from the direction of Konjević-Polje to Cerska, to the place of execution. Construction machinery followed the convoy.

More than 6,000 people were detained in three locations in the municipality of Bratunac.

The majority were transported to the town of Bratunac, the rest were detained in the warehouse of the Agricultural Cooperative in Kravica. The prisoners were robbed of their money, watches, and jewellery. The shooting started around 6 p.m. and lasted until the next morning. Policemen and soldiers occasionally entered the warehouse, shooting or throwing hand grenades through windows. In the morning, the Serb soldiers asked the survivors to come out from the warehouse for medical help. Everyone who answered this call was immediately killed.

School in Grbavci

In the evening of 13th July, Vujadin Popović informed his subordinates in the Zvornik Brigade that a large number of prisoners from Bratunac were to arrive in their territory. He told Drago Nikolić, Zvornik Brigade Security Officer, that the prisoners were being brought into the municipality of Zvornik to be executed. That same night, a convoy of six buses arrived at the school in Grbavci in the village of Orahovci, near Zvornik. The next morning, the remaining prisoners were sent on their way towards Zvornik in a convoy of overcrowded buses. The conditions were terrible, with some people collapsing due to the heat, exhaustion induced by hunger and lack of air. Those that tried to escape were killed.

When entering the sports hall, the prisoners were forced to leave personal belongings and clothes in a pile in front of the school. Around noon the Zvornik Brigade engineering units started digging a large pit in a field not far from the school. First, they forced the prisoners into the dressing room, where their hands were tied and their eyes blindfolded. Then each prisoner was given a cup of water to drink. A huge pit was now already waiting in the field one kilometre away from the school. They lined them up next to the pit and shot them.

"*Babo*, where are you?"

One of the members of the Zvornik Brigade, who later testified about the executions in Grbavci, told the International Criminal Tribunal for the former Yugoslavia about what happened after the shooting:

"From that pile, that heap of dead bodies that did not resemble human bodies any more, a human being emerged. I said human being but it was actually a boy, five or six years old. It was unbelievable. Unbelievable. A human being came out and started walking towards a path, a path along which men were standing doing their job, carrying automatic rifles. (...) And then, out of nowhere they all put their guns down and all of them were just paralysed. And it was only a child in front of them. If it were a person in his 70ies or 80ies it would be terrifying enough, let alone an innocent, sweet child. And this child was covered in the tissue and intestines of other humans. (...) And this child emerged from the pile of executed people, calling: 'Babo'... this is their word for father. The boy said: '*Babo*, where are you?'"

Mevludin Orić, who survived the execution, described the killings:

"My cousin was immediately hit. He cried out for help, gripping my hand tightly. I let go of his hand and threw myself on the ground. He fell over me. He fell over my spine. From that moment on I pretended to be dead. For some time he was sort of shivering on top of me and then just became paralysed. He died lying on top of me. Some other men from the group could be heard, two or three of them started crying for help because of their wounds. Then those people would come over to finished them off. This is how it continued, bringing them in, killing."

Red Mud

The other group of prisoners from Bratunac was taken to the village of Petkovac near Zvornik on 14th July and also located in the village school. They were imprisoned in over-crowded classrooms on both floors of the school.

Guards confiscated any money and personal documents that the prisoners possessed. There was no water, nor were they allowed to open windows or use the toilet. From time to time, guards entered the classrooms, separated some of the men and killed them.

The next morning, the prisoners were taken out in front of the school and ordered to take off their shoes and most of their clothes. Then their hands were tied behind their backs and they were put on trucks. Red Mud Dam is located three kilometres away from the school. They drove the prisoners to the field near the dam and a whole day of shooting began. After lining up the victims, RS Army soldiers shot them in the back or head from a distance of 10 metres. Then one soldier would check on the victims and shoot those who were only wounded in the head.

No One Was Begging for Their Life

The third group of detainees was transported to the village of Ročević, in the territory of Kozluk. The next day, on 15th July, the execution started. Detainees were blindfolded, their hands were tied, and they were put into the trucks and driven to the gravel pit in Kozluk.

Veljko Ivanović, a Zvornik Brigade member who took part in the transportation of prisoners, later stated during the trial at the International Criminal Tribunal for the former Yugoslavia: "They were half dead, exhausted, without water, without bread. No one asked for their life to be spared or begged. Not anyone. This worried me. No one said: 'Save my life!'"

The Village of Kula

The fourth group of detainees from Bratunac was transferred to the village of Kula, on the road between Zvornik and Bijeljina. They were detained in the classrooms of the Secondary School. On the morning of 16th July, they were transferred to Branjevo Military Farm. They were transported in groups of ten, with their hands tied behind their backs, with some men blindfolded, and put on buses.

During the same morning, a unit of the 10th Sabotage Detachment under the command of Brano Gojković received orders to go to the Military Farm in Branjevo. From 10.00 a.m. until the early afternoon of that day, eight members of 10th Sabotage Detachment executed around 1.500 detainees. According to the testimony of Dražen Erdemović, a soldier of the 10th Sabotage Detachment, prisoners with blindfolds around their heads and bound hands were taken off of the buses in groups and killed at a distance of about a hundred metres.

In the Cultural Centre of a place called Pilica, there were around 500 men detained.

Bratunac brigade soldiers who had arrived in Branjevo that afternoon volunteered to perform further executions.

The process of hiding and destroying evidence of the crimes committed started at the same time as the mass executions. The majority of the work was done by the engineering units of the RS Army.

Operation "Sanitation"

The operation performed by RS civilian and military authorities to erase any traces, and cover up the crimes committed was given the code name "Sanitation", a term meaning hygienic and sanitary measures carried out in a warzone. The criminal operation of transferring the bodies from the execution sites to smaller, so-called 'secondary graves', was supposed to be secret, but eventually required the support of civilian resources and the manpower of local sanitation companies from Bratunac and Zvornik,

since military resources were insufficient.

Covering up and destroying evidence of the genocide in Srebrenica was the largest operation of this kind in the territory of former Yugoslavia, including similar operations undertaken by the Serbian Ministry of Interior in Kosovo in 1999. Until March 2009, when the search for missing persons was handed over to the authorities of Bosnia and Herzegovina, the Office of the Prosecutor of the International Criminal Tribunal for the former Yugoslavia and the International Commission on Missing Persons had discovered 73 mass graves of victims from Srebrenica: 31 primary graves, 37 secondary graves, and five mass graves where no information was available.

The Transfer of Bodies

After the first burial, an operation to transfer the bodies of victims from the primary grave

Reburials

"When I returned from Krajina on 20th October, I learned that several members of the Engineering Unit of the brigade, some military police, and Drago Nikolić were involved in the reburial of prisoners who had been killed in July 1995. The others involved were taken over by Popović, including some of the members of the Drina Corps military police who secured the area and controlled the traffic at the sites of reburial. I have also heard that during this operation Popović wore civilian clothes, and that groundwork machinery and manpower from the Zvornik Brigade was used in the first burial and excavation, but have no information as to whether they were also involved in the making of secondary graves. I have also heard that Popović and Drago Nikolić changed truck drivers intermittently and that some members of the Engineering Unit of the Zvornik Brigade loaded corpses from the primary graves. Apparently, Popović and Beara supervised the works during the operation of reburial, and wore civilian clothes."

(Statement on the extensive operation to remove and transfer the remains of the Srebrenica victims by Major Dragan Obrenović.)

sites started in autumn 1995. On 14th September 1995, the RS Army headquarters approved five tons of diesel fuel for the Drina Corps Command for "engineering works". The fuel was supposed to be delivered to Captain Milorad Trbić, Deputy Chief of Security of the Zvornik Brigade.

The exhumation and transfer of corpses from Glogova to Zeleni Jadar, in the territory of the Bratunac Brigade, took place by night. Momir Nikolić, the Bratunac Brigade's Assistant Commander for Security and Intelligence, admitted before the ICTY that he had coordinated the action of exhumation and reburial during the period from the mid-September to October, 1995.

"Everything was done in cooperation with the military police of the Bratunac Brigade, the civilian police and members of the 5th Engineering Battalion of the Drina Corps. I reported at the command meeting of the Bratunac Brigade in October 1995, in front of the assembled officers of command (...) that we received the order from the RS Army Headquarters to complete the operation to transfer Muslim corpses."

The exhumation and transportation of bodies from the primary gravesites, located within the zone of responsibility of the Zvornik Brigade, took place over a period of several nights in September and October 1995. The operation was headed by Milorad Trbić.

Network of Gravesites

There is ample evidence, including vital forensic evidence, proving the connection between the execution sites, the primary graves, and the network of secondary gravesites.

The victims of the first mass execution in Cerska were found in mass graves near Nova Kasaba. Forensic evidence did not leave any doubt that the victims were civilians who were tied and bound at the time of execution. Through the forensic examination of the warehouse in Kravica, the ICTY investigation team discovered clear traces of human blood, bones, and tissue on the walls, floor, and ceiling, along with evidence of damage caused by weapons and explosives. It was this forensic evidence that made it possible to connect this execution site with the secondary graves.

The remains of around 1.300 persons were found in primary and secondary graves connected to the mass executions at the warehouse in Kravica. Among the remains exhumed from the primary gravesite near the dam in Petkovci and the secondary gravesites connected to it, 805 bodies were identified as persons reported missing. It is agreed that over 800 people were killed in 1995 in Petkovci.

In the morning of 16th July 1995, Dragan Jokić, Chief of Engineering of the Zvornik Brigade, ordered his subordi-

nates to go to Kozluk to bury bodies. At the execution site, they found pits full of bodies and broken glass from the nearby factory. Since there was not enough equipment on hand to bury the bodies, civilian machinery was brought in, in order to accomplish the burial. Forensic evidence connected six secondary graves with this primary grave in Kozluk. Through DNA analysis, 1.040 persons who were reported missing after the fall of Srebrenica have been identified from amongst the remains exhumed from the primary grave in Kozluk and associated secondary graves,

The transportation and burial of the bodies from the executions in the Cultural Centre in Pilica started on the same day immediately following the executions. The Zvornik Brigade soldiers loaded the bodies on to two trucks.

During the morning of 17th July, members of the Zvornik Brigade Engineering Troop dug

Death Squad

"Lieutenant Colonel Brano Gojković took us to a farm. I didn't know the name of that farm. (...) I knew that the village of Pilica was nearby, but it was only when we got there that I learned what was happening that day. They told us that buses of civilians would come from Srebrenica. (...) The buses started arriving. They took out people in groups of ten. They took them to the meadow. We started shooting at those people. I don't know exactly, to be honest, I couldn't follow, it was simply ... I don't know. I felt sick. I had a headache. I tried to avoid it as much as I could, to avoid taking part in it. I wanted to save one man, but they would not let me. This man told me that he had helped Serbs leave Srebrenica and go to the Federal Republic of Yugoslavia. So I grabbed on to this, the fact that this man had helped, but it didn't help. They told me... it was Brano who had said he wanted no witness to the crime. I kept silent. Then a group of soldiers from Bratunac arrived. They were just taking out their frustration on those people. They beat them with iron bars. They cursed them. No-one from our group beat them, but Savanović Stav... Stanko and Brano stood out amongst the others killing those people (...) After that, around 3 o'clock, I don't know the exact time, but I believe it was around 3.00 p.m. – this Lieutenant Colonel came again together with those two military policemen and he told us that in the Cultural Centre in that place Pilica there were – he said the number, and that is why I mention this number too – that there were around 500 Muslim prisoners who were about to break out and flee. I said that I no longer wished to execute them and that I am not a robot for killing. I should also tell you this. If any-one had told me at that moment that I had to kill the Lieutenant Colonel, I would have done so. Three of my colleagues stood by me and also refused to go. So then they gave up the idea and left. However, those people from Bratunac... we still hadn't left that farm, when we heard shots and explosions from the Centre. Then Bra-no Gojković said that the Lieutenant Colonel had told us to come to a meeting. The meeting took place in a cafe across from the Cultural Centre. The Lieutenant Colonel didn't say anything in particular... Actually I wasn't pay-ing attention to what he was saying. I wasn't interested at all. So, while I was there in that cafe, I was just listen-ing to those shots and explosions. After that, the peo-ple from Bratunac came to the cafe, and the Lieutenant Colonel said that we were finished and that he wanted to talk to them alone. So, we got up and left. I said that I wanted to go home to see my child. That was it. So we went back to Vlasenica and in the evening they took us to Bijeljina by buses."

(Testimony by Dražen Erdemović, soldier of the 10th Sabotage Detachment of the Bosnian Serb Army.)

a pit at the Military Farm. The bodies were then loaded on to the trucks by employees of the local utility company and the Civil Defence. Among the remains exhumed from the primary grave in the Branjevo Military Farm and associated secondary graves, 960 bodies were identified as persons reported missing after the fall of Srebrenica, through DNA analysis. It is estimated that between 1,000 and 2,000 people were killed on 16th July 1995 in the area of Pilica (at the Branjevo Military Farm and the Cultural Centre in Pilica).

THE GUILT

Information about the Genocide

One month after the fall of Srebrenica, on 11th August 1995, the United States Ambassador to the United Nations, Madeleine Albright, presented the global public with evidence on the crimes committed, which included satellite images of recently excavated mass graves in Nova Kasaba. After this shocking discovery and the resultant brief period of concern among the international community, nothing happened. About twenty days later, there was another massacre at the Sarajevo open market, 'Markale', resulting in 43 civilian deaths. It was only after this second event, that NATO launched air strikes against RS Army positions and the military infrastructure at the end of August 1995. By September, the RS military and political leadership, faced with a complete military breakdown across the entire country of Bosnia and Herzegovina, withdrew heavy artillery from around Sarajevo beyond the city reach and agreed to negotiations to end the war.

Peace negotiations in Dayton, USA, started at the beginning of November 1995 and were concluded by the end of the month, ending the aggression against Bosnia and Herzegovina after four years.

Sentencing

In 1993, the UN Security Council established the International Criminal Tribunal for the former Yugoslavia – ICTY - as a response to the mass killings, ethnic cleansing and other se-

Yasushi Akashi, UN Secretary General Special Envo[y]
for the former Yugoslavia, and Radovan Karadž[ić]

rious violations of international humanitarian law committed in the former Yugoslavia. This court indicted Radovan Karadžić, the President of the Republika Srpska, and Ratko Mladić, Commander-in-Chief of the RS Army, responsible for the genocide in Srebrenica.

Karadžić was arrested 13 years later, on 21st July 2008, and Mladić in May 2011, after 16 years of hiding in Serbia and the Republika Srpska. In the first instance, the court found Karadžić guilty of genocide in Srebrenica and sentenced him to 40 years' of imprisonment. Mladić's trial is still in process.

This Court convicted General Radislav Krstić for genocide in 2001, and sentenced him to 46 years' imprisonment. Four years later, his sentence was reduced to 35 years' imprisonment for aiding and supporting genocide. This was the first conviction for genocide given by the Hague Tribunal.

Former RS Army officers Vu-jadin Popović and Ljubiša Beara were sentenced to life-imprisonment in The Hague in June 2010 for the genocide of Bosniaks in Srebrenica. At the same time, five more officers from the RS Army and police have also been sentenced: Drago Nikolić to 35 years' imprisonment, Ljubomir Borovčanin to 17 years, Vinko Pandurević to 13 years, Radivoje Miletić to 18 years, and Milan Gvero to five years.

In December 2012, the International Criminal Tribunal for the former Yugoslavia convicted General Zdravko Tolimir, ex-assistant to Ratko Mladić and war Chief of the Intelligence Service of the RS Army Supreme Command, finding him guilty of genocide and sentencing him to life-imprisonment.

For crimes in Srebrenica, the ICTY also convicted former RS Army officers Momir Nikolić to 20 years' imprisonment, Vidoje Blagojević to 15 years, Dragan Obrenović to 17, and Dragan Jokić to nine years'

"He was tall and died horribly"

In spite of the interest caused by Madeleine Albright's report to the United Nations, only one journalist followed-up on the images –*The Boston Globe* reporter, David Rohde. Rohde, who was also arrested during his research, and has written an awarded book about this entitled *Endgame: The Betrayal and Fall of Srebrenica* and thus significantly contributed to the timely discovery of the real extent of the crimes committed in Srebrenica.

"In the soft early morning light, surrounded by peaceful green fields and wild flowers, massacres seemed impossible (...) I reached the dirt path and saw what looked like some clothes in the distance. The clothes, an empty cloth bag, some pieces of paper, a bullet, and Muslim prayer beads lay scattered across the grass. Dozens of the papers had *Srebrenica* stamped on them.

I grabbed the prayer beads, the bullet, and the scraps of paper and headed back to the car (...) Back at the car, I headed down the steep embankment to check the small field next to the river where earlier I had spotted an area of fresh digging. To my left, something white jutted from a 20 foot by 20 foot plot of freshly dug earth. Two long, thin bones, one the size and shape of a human femur, the other of a human tibia, stared up at me (...) I checked the last field, looked at the bones one last time, picked up some shell casings from the side of the road, and got in the car. As I sped north toward the border, despair washed over me. He must have been tall, I thought, and he must have died horribly."

imprisonment. The Court of Bosnia and Herzegovina continued the process of prosecution of their subordinates, those directly responsible for crimes. In the final judgement of Bosnia and Herzegovina's action against the then Federal Republic of Yugoslavia at the International Court of Justice in The Hague (ICJ), twelve years after the crimes in Srebrenica the ICJ concurred that, with the support of the Republic of Serbia, "Bosnian Serbs planned and executed the genocide in Srebrenica".

Genocide Denial

In spite of incontestable evidence and final judgments by the highest international legal institutions, the State of Serbia and the Bosnian entity, the Republika Srpska, continue to systematically deny the Srebrenica genocide. The long history of official denial and silence surrounding the genocide started with the so-called 'Report on the Srebrenica Case' prepared by the RS Bureau for Cooperation with the ICJ, which was adopted by the RS Government during the mandate of Mladen Ivanić. The report completely denied the massacre and accused the International Committee of the Red Cross of forging the evidence of killings. In international legal circles, this report was considered as "one of the worst cases of revisionism".

This did not discourage the RS Government: in March 2008, they decided to financially support the organisation "The Stitching Srebrenica Historical Project" which was based in The Hague, and established with the aim of denying the legally established facts about the genocide. The RS Government made available "all technical and administrative help" to this organisation. As a result, during the period from 2008 to 2014, "The Stitching Srebrenica Historical Project" received almost two million convertible

marks from the RS Government's budget. The President of the Srebrenica Historical Project, Stefan Karganović, is infamous for his claims that less than 1,000 people were killed in Eastern Bosnia in July 1995.

American publicist Michael Dobbs wrote in the *Foreign Policy* magazine that this sort of sponsorship could be compared with the unrealistic scenario of "the German Government and Parliament annually allocating state funds for research by David Irving and other revisionist holocaust historians". Despite the fact that responsibility for the Srebrenica genocide is well established, the Republic of Serbia is still denying its role in the crime. Only under pressure from the international community – which required the implementation of obligations implied by the judgment of the ICJ to condemn the genocide in Srebrenica – did the Parliament of Serbia adopt a symbolic declaration in which it "strongly condemns the crime committed against the Bosnian Muslim population of Srebrenica in July 1995, as determined by the ruling of the International Court of Justice".

The Status of Srebrenica Today

Today, Srebrenica is a municipality within the B&H entity of the Republika Srpska. It is inhabited by no more than 7,000 permanent residents. It does not have any special status within the entity of Republika Srpska. The pre-war economy is almost entirely destroyed. Apart from one pre-war factory in Potočari with significantly smaller capacities than before, Srebrenica's economy relies mostly on public funding. The majority of the employed population works in the public sector, the municipality, schools, and public enterprises. Three or four private factories located at the town entrance are all that is left of the pre-war industry.

Infrastructure, residential buildings and houses have been rebuilt to a large extent, but their reconstruction does not necessarily imply the return of the population. The majority of expelled Srebrenica citizens still live around Tuzla, Sarajevo or abroad. The only permanent guardians of this part of the country are those buried in Potočari. For them, Srebrenica remains "the only place where they could go while alive and the only place they couldn't leave because they are dead".

Survivors from Srebrenica were resettled with the full support of state institutions and the international community. The majority were resettled in the surrounding area of Tuzla and on the periphery of Sarajevo. In the year 2000, their number started to decrease in both areas; with the majority leaving Bosnia and Herzegovina, and only a small number trying to return to their pre-war homes.

Serbia's Responsibility

There is abundant evidence of the aggression of the then Federal Republic of Yugoslavia against Bosnia and Herzegovina. Rulings of the International Court of Justice in The Hague (ICJ) confirmed beyond doubt numerous cases of the direct and indirect involvement of the official Army of FRY in military operations in Bosnia and Herzegovina. In the case of Srebrenica, the ruling states that the Federal Republic of Yugoslavia (FRY) – whose legal successor is the Republic of Serbia – provided significant military and financial support to the Republika Srpska and was to a large extent "in a position to influence the Bosnian Serbs who devised and implemented the genocide in Srebrenica".

The 30th Personnel Centre of the Yugoslav Army General Staff was established in November 1993 by the Chief of the General Staff of the Yugoslav Army, Momčilo Perišić.

The Centre was established in order to provide military and logistical support, regulate salary payments and the status of a large number of Yugoslav Army officers who served in the RS Army or were transferred from the Yugoslav Army to the RS Army. It is therefore a fact that the Centre was in charge of the Republika Srpska, and this fact leaves no doubt about the effective control of the Yugoslav Army over the RS Army. The 30th Personnel Centre continued to exist right up until 28 February 2002, when the Serbian Government decided upon its closure, as one of the conditions for Serbia's accession to the NATO Partnership for Peace programme. Therefore the financing of the RS Army by Serbia formally ceased at that time.

Another proof of Serbia's aggression against Bosnia and Herzegovina is the General Framework Agreement for Peace in Bosnia and Herzegovina, signed at the USA air force base, Wright-Patterson in the city of Dayton in 1995. The countries' signatories to this peace agreement were: the Republic of Bosnia and Herzegovina, the Republic of Croatia, and the Federal Republic of Yugoslavia (FRY). Since peace agreements are signed between the warring parties, Slobodan Milošević's signature on the Dayton Peace Agreement constitutes a formal acknowledgement of the aggression by FRY (i.e. Serbia) against Bosnia and Herzegovina.

Secret Actions of Serbian Police

In accordance with the orders of the Deputy Minister of the Interior of the RS, Tomislav Kovač, dated 10th July 1995, "a mixed company of joint forces of the Ministry of Interior of the Republic of Srpska Krajina (RSK), Serbia, and Republika Srpska" was transferred from Trnovo to the area of Srebrenica and placed under the command of Ljubomir Borovčanin

Evidence on the Participation of the FRY in Genocide

In its judgement dated 26 February 2007, in the legal action of Bosnia and Herzegovina against the Federal Republic of Yugoslavia, the International Court of Justice in The Hague stated:

"There is much evidence of direct or indirect participation by the official army of the FRY, along with the Bosnian Serb armed forces, in military operations in Bosnia and Herzegovina in the years prior to the events at Srebrenica.

FRY made its considerable military and financial support available to the Republika Srpska, and had it withdrawn that support, this would have greatly constrained the options that were available to the Republika Srpska authorities; one of the forms of that support was payment of salaries and other benefits to officers of the RS Army.

In July 1995, Serbia was in a position of influence over the Bosnian Serbs who devised and implemented the genocide in Srebrenica, unlike that of any of the other states party to the Genocide Convention owing to the strength of the political, military and financial links between the FRY on the one hand and the Republika Srpska and the RS Army on the other;

Serbia violated its obligation to prevent the Srebrenica genocide in such a manner as to engage its international responsibility."

*(Excerpt from the judgement
by the International Court of Justice in The Hague.)*

Republika Srbija

MINISTARSTVO UNUTRAŠNJIH POSLOVA
SEKRETARIJAT U UŽICU
OUP BAJINA BAŠTA
Broj:28-744
23.07.1995.godine
Bajina Bašta

01193951

Z A P I S N I K

O izvršenoj primopredaji lica i stvari u OUP-a Bajina Bašta

Dana 23.07.1995.godine u _18 oc_ časova u OUP-a Bajina Bašta izvršena je primo
predaja lica muslimanske nacionalnosti koji su izbegli iz Srebrenice, a ilegalno
su prešli državnu granicu iz Republike Srpske na teritoriju SRJ.

Primopredaja je izvršena izmedju radnika OUP-a Bajina Bašta, koji su izvršili
predaju i radnika SJB Skelani, RS, koji su izvršili prijem lica u dalju nadlež

Ovom prilikom predata su lica koja su ilegalno prešla državnu granicu pomoću
čamca preko Drine iz pravca Bjelovca,opština Bratunac, na područje Vrhpolja
opština Ljubovija, a radi se o sledećim licima:

1. SALIHOVIĆ SADIK od oca Hakije, rodjen 26.06.1965.godine u Srebrenici
gde je i živeo.Kod sebe nije imao ličnih isprava niti drugog ličnog prtljaga
osim odevnih predmeta. Prilikom pretresa kod njega je pronadjen pištolj marke
"Zastava", fabrički broj 21987, kal. 7,65 mm, sa 5 metaka u okviru istog
kalibra i jedan nož sa kožnim futrolom

2. DELIĆ HAMDIJA od oca Ahme rodjen 25.05.1972 gdine u Srebrenici gde je
živeo. Sa sobom je nosio jednu ručnu bombu koja je naknadno pronadjena na
desnoj obali drine u selu Vrhpolju na mestu gde je izvršio ilegalanxprelazak
Bomba fabrički broj 7202. Kod sebe nije imao drugog ličnog prtljag ani ti
ličnih isprava sem odevnih predmeta.

Opisana lica predata radnicima SJB Skelani od strane radnika OUP-a Bajine
Baša u dalju nadležnost. S obzirom da su ilegalno ušli u SRJ , da nema inte
resa za dalju operativnu obradu, da nemaju važeću putnu ispravu ili vizu
trećih zemalja.

LICA I STVARI PRIMIO   O V E R A V A   LICA I STVARI PRED
za SJB SKELANI   KOMANDIR SM B.BAŠTA   ZA OUP B.BAŠTA
OSL Milun Perendić   Slavko Petrović   Milovan Jevtović

П. С. Наведена лица су преузета без наведених личних ствари.
(оружија)

"Minutes of the Meeting" from the Ministry of the Republic of
Serbia on the "handover of Muslims" to the RS police

"in order to break the enemy offensive from the protected zone of Srebrenica".

This order clearly shows participation of forces from the Serbian Ministry of the Interior in operations in and around Srebrenica, although this was a long kept secret. Obviously, it was impossible for Serbian police to be in Bosnia and Herzegovina (first in Trnovo and then in Srebrenica) without the knowledge and approval of the top political authorities in Serbia, or more precisely, Slobodan Milošević. Colonel Ljubomir Borovcanin was appointed by Kovač as the Commander of all police forces in Srebrenica. At the end of June and the beginning of July 1995, two reports that he prepared reveal that the three units of Serbian special police forces were under his command long before their transfer to Srebrenica on 10th July.

In his report, sent to the police force headquarters in Pale, dated 30th June 1995,

Borovčanin states that his troops, the Special Police Brigade and "the police detachment 'Kajman' (MoI, Serbia)" attacked "object Lučevik", a day before, but without success. Complaining about bad intelligence data, Borovčanin states that the attack "turned into a violent patrolling", and that in this attack two men from his brigade were wounded, as well as two members of the "MoI of Serbia".

In his next report sent on 1st July, Borovčanin stated that two platoons from the 'Kajman' detachment, 'the Plavi' and 'the Scorpions' (MoI of Serbia)" took part in the conflicts of the previous day.

The Serbian police force was present in Trnovo at least five more days. On 6th July, Tomislav Kovač sent a daily report to all police stations in the Serb areas of Sarajevo stating among others things, that "special units of MoI of RS, Serbia, and RSK" are still attacking the "Lisičija Glava point".

Four days later, he signed orders to send Borovčanin to Srebrenica, together with mixed units of the MoI from the RS, RSK, and Serbia, commanding them to be in Bratunac by noon on 11th July. A document dated from 24th July exposes the fact that two out of three Serbian units were in Srebrenica.

"The night on the Trnovo front line was peaceful, Special Police Force Banja Luka troop took over the shift from the MoI Serbia unit, the Scorpions". Savo Cvijetinović, who assumed command for the police forces in Borovčanin's absence, said that day in his report. However, two other units, "Plavi" and "Kajman", were not replaced from the shift that day. Moreover, they were not there by the end of July, but in the surroundings of Srebrenica.

The Responsibility of the UN

There are few such large-scale crimes as the one committed in Srebrenica, where the world had direct insight to it and the instruments to stop it, yet did nothing. There is no doubt that the genocide in Srebrenica could have been prevented. A debate about the responsibility of the UN or in other words, of the command of the Dutch Battalion, is on-going. UN Resolution 819 declared Srebrenica a "UN Safe Zone" and the UN was obligated to protect it. Lack of interest or open obstruction by the UN officials resulted in the physical extinction of a large part of the Bosniak community in Eastern Bosnia.

Yasushi Akashi, a Japanese diplomat and UN Secretary General Special Envoy for the former Yugoslavia during the fall of Srebrenica and French General Bernard Janvier, Commander of UNPROFOR for former Yugoslavia, prevented the bombing of RS Army positions on the morning of 11th July 1995. In spite of its clearly defined mission to pro-

Philippe Morillon, Commander of the UNPROFOR forces in B&H, who promised UN protection of the citizens of Srebrenica

tect the "safe zone" of Srebrenica, the Dutch Battalion stood aside. Deputy Battalion Commander Robert Franken even contributed to covering up the crimes. After leaving the enclave he withheld a list of the 242 men who were in the battery factory, which was the only proof that they were alive, despite the fact that he promised some of the victim's relatives that he would send the list to all international human-rights organisations.

The Dutch attitude towards Srebrenica has long been an issue of internal political relations, the balance of forces in the Parliament or the Government itself. All investigations so far on the role of the Netherlands in Srebrenica have resulted in diminishing the importance that the Dutch Battalion had in the enclave. Such investigations in most cases ended in pardoning their own soldiers for the errors they made, in passively observing the crime committed in front of their eyes. The Dutch Government, presided over by Wim Kok, resigned in 2003 after the Dutch Institute for War Documentation published its findings on the Dutch responsibility for Srebrenica.

None of the United Nations high officials was ever called to account for genocide in Srebrenica.

My Srebrenica

Even the nettle grows here no more,
Nor the violet, nor the wallflower:
Here the earth is painful,
Dark blue like the sky.

No one works on the fields any more
No mowing, nor plowing!

This is where in daylong conversations
bones are joined with white swallows – the shadows.

And whoever comes mentions us.

O my Srebrenica, dear Srebrenica,
Srebrenica wishes, you are my hope,
Srebrenica bleeds, blood of my kin,
I will be back, we shall all come back,
My native soil!

Srebrenica Inferno (2001), Džemaludin Latić

REMEMBRANCE

The Great Harvest of Death

When you put the shovel down, and someone takes over and continues instead of you, you take a look at a tombstone and realise that – well, yes, you know him, and you feel ashamed again because you're not able to recall his character to your memory, in the same way as you're not able to recall to your memory the characters of so many of them – all better than yourself. When you find yourself at the grave at the same time as the mother of one of them, she asks you: "Were you a friend of his?"; you lie that you were, when actually you weren't; he only protected you once from the other boys worse than yourself, and was nice to you and would smile at you when passing by, and so you lie, and you know that his smiles are reason enough for you to weep, and you know that all of his best friends are dead, that it's only you left together with a few others, equally irrelevant: you have arrived at Potočari.

Your feelings are redundant, you shouldn't have the right to be sad, and really you should be ashamed. This is the feeling that shall probably be interwoven into everything you'll do for the rest of your life, something you will feel every time you're thirsty, when you're hungry, when you go shopping, when you fall in love, when you're unhappy or when you wish to have children – you will always feel ashamed. Ashamed that on that day you didn't have enough strength to go with them, for thinking at least once that you might escape: for the selfish thought that you have deserved to live; you shall readily bear this blame, since this is all you've got to remember them.

While walking around these open graves, you know that this is the last chance to make peace with them, that maybe you will move on with their permission, start living again, after you tell them everything you wanted to tell them while they were alive; at least to those you knew or those who knew about them. And then, while caressing the smooth surface of a coffin or looking at someone doing this, you realise that this is not possible – not because of what you have shared with them, but for what you haven't. Then, without any grain of doubt you realise that the only future you have belongs to them; probably because in order to have a future you have to have someone to share the past with. Only when you realise how meaningless life without them is going to be, do you realise how meaninglessly unnecessary their death was, how stupidly meaningless.

The dull sound of wet soil shovelled on to the wooden boards in the vaults feels like blows; forcefully the turf falls, covering up parts of your life, and ultimately filling in the holes from the impact of shells, bullets, and knifes. However, what will remain once the earth has settled is a desert; even if you wish, you know that you shall not be able to move on, because anything you're going to feel after this, everything beyond this, will be worn-out, ragged, and superficial. This is why you will be deceiving everyone around you for the rest of your life, all those women, men, and children, because you'll never feel for them the way you used to feel about those other people, and no one will ever be as im-

portant to you. So you will cheat on them with the dead. The air is still plagued here, as if someone had opened the window onto a worse past. This is actually a problem of survival: the past is supposed to seem like a better place. You had this same feeling then, moving through a vast crowd that emerged, seeming as if it had no end to it; nothing changed in their faces, they are still shaped with pain, red from crying. And you still dream about the same people, tell the same stories, look at the same photographs smeared by fingertips – that is if you still have them – but none of those in the pictures are still alive.

Yes, opportunities sometimes arise, people approach unexpectedly, but they are only shadows left after the great harvest of death. You meet knowing that it will not be joint graduation photos you'll hang on the wall, but photos of the graves of mutual friends. You have actually graduated before death: many failed, some passed, but no one was left intact. And you are sure, dead sure, their graves are the only place you will reunite, at least once, and find each other in the multitude. These are actually the only moments when you can talk about everyday things without a guilty conscience, because this place is in some bizarre way better than everything that's left. In any other place and on any other occasion your conversation would stumble, be difficult, different worlds to which you now belong would stand between you. Not here though; here you are in the place from which you set off, together with those who now lie around you.

It is probably with this same feeling of shame that you realise: even if you move on there's nowhere to go. You would prefer to stay there, to sleep among the tombstones. Perhaps because you're selfish; certainly partly because when you turn your back on them, there is so much evidence that everything is wrong, that you're not important, that the judgement day shall never come, because it has already passed by, and there is no place for anything in you, that you only feel fine when the situation is at its worst, because no one you know can experience anything better. You approach those caskets once again, you bow down and touch the heavy covering of soil; you tap the caskets like a lunatic, first one then another, on and on, you are saying goodbye, still tapping, until the earth covers your palms and dries on your fingertips. This is all you can take away from here. Hours later you open your fists and one drop of sweat, black as that soil, slips away down your palm.

And you will start crying. You cannot even wipe away the tears, they're coming harder and saltier, cascading down your cheeks burning as if penetrating the skin, never to stop, because you feel as if they were killed on this very day and this long delayed death is actually much harder. You want to cry out for all of them and after all of them, and for all those years in which you clenched your teeth afraid of that familiar shiver of the jaw. Perhaps you're right, because they're not unknown corpses scattered throughout the woods any more, today their stolen dignity is returned, today they have their names again, their pasts, sisters, brothers, wives and children, their parents. And I guess this is why you cry: you have known them as they were, and lost them. And today, when they again became who they used to be, you don't have them anymore.

Emir Suljagić

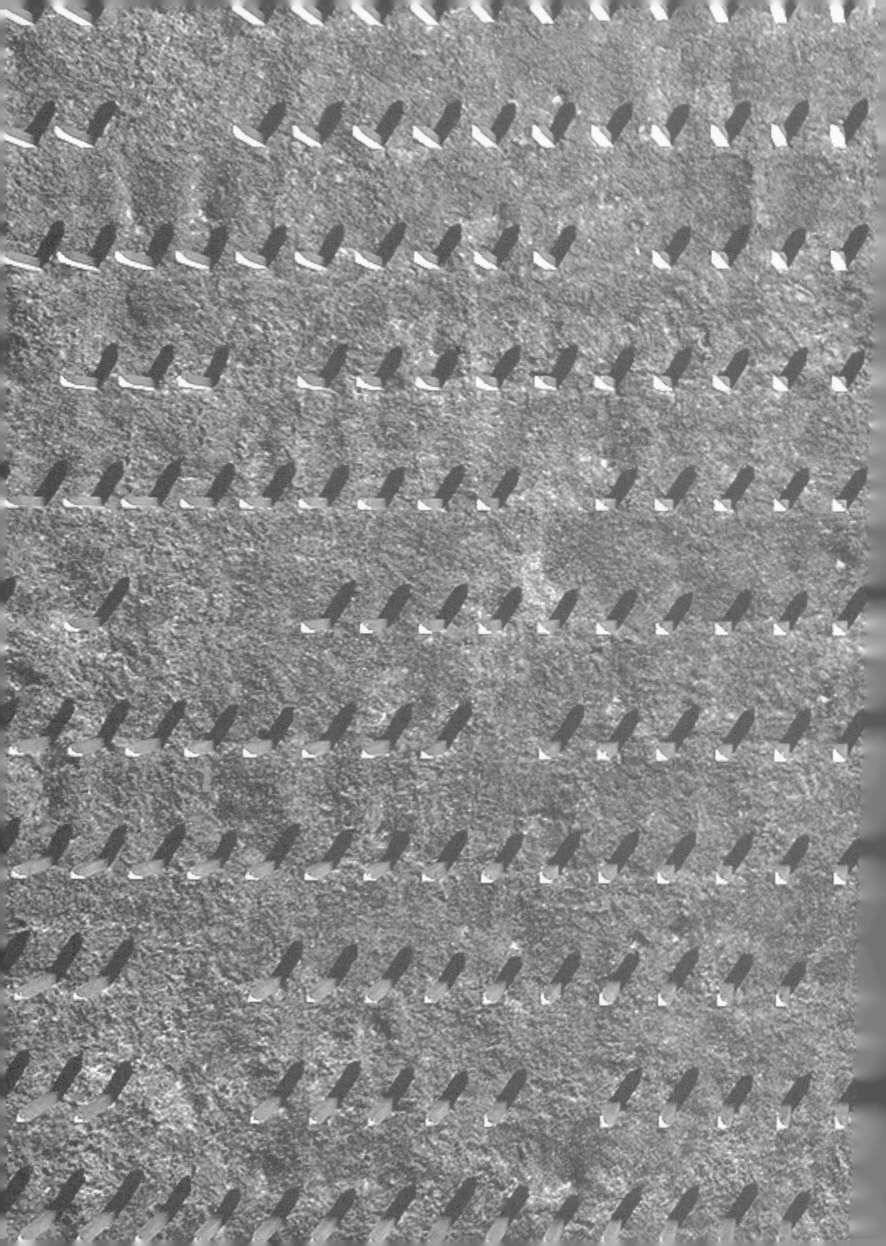

THE DIRECTORY

Akashi, Yasushi – UN Secretary General's Special Envoy to the former Yugoslavia. He was strongly criticized for his role in the process, particularly for failing to enforce the safety of civilians in safe zones, and for his role in the genocide operation in Srebrenica.

Annan, Koffi – Head of Department or Under-Secretary-General for UN peace operations from 1993 to 1995. He was Head of Department during the collapse of the peace mission in Somalia and during the genocides in Rwanda and Bosnia and Herzegovina. Canadian general Romeo Dallaire, who commanded the UN forces in Rwanda, accused him of preventing the UN from intervening. The same can be claimed for Annan's actions during the genocide operation in Srebrenica.

Beara, Ljubiša – Colonel and Chief of Security of the RS Army Main Staff. In the trial before the ICTY he was sentenced to life-imprisonment for genocide, complicity to commit genocide, crimes against humanity, and violation of the laws or customs of war. The verdict against him states that he had the clearest overall picture of the massive scale and scope of the killing operation. From his presence in Bratunac on the night of 13th July, to his personal visits to the various detention and execution sites, as well as the significant logistical challenges he faced throughout, Beara had a very personal view of the staggering number of victims destined for execution. Beara became, in the opinion of the Trial Chamber, "a driving force behind the murder enterprise".

Blagojević, Vidoje – Commander of the Bratunac Brigade of the RS Army. Found guilty by the ICTY for aiding and abetting the extermination and persecutions on political, racial and religious grounds, and sentenced to 15 years' imprisonment.

Borovčanin, Ljubomir – Deputy Commander of the Republika Srpska Ministry of Internal Affairs (MoI) Special Police Brigade. From 10th July 1995, Commander of Joint Forces of the Ministry of Interior, and subordinate to the Drina Corps of the RS Army during his participation in the Srebrenica operation. Found guilty for aiding and abetting crimes against humanity and violation of the laws or customs of war, and sentenced to 17 years' imprisonment.

Boškić, Marko – member of the 10th Sabotage Detachment of the RS Army General Staff. He pleaded guilty to persecution and murder in the trial before the Court of Bosnia and Herzegovina. He was sentenced to 10 years' imprisonment. Before the trial, he had been living in the United States of America.

Boutros Boutros-Ghali – United Nations Secretary General from January 1992 to December 1996. As a result of his incapability to mobilise support within the UN, the United States of America vetoed his second mandate. His passivity failed to stop the genocides in Rwanda and Bosnia and Herzegovina. He personally obstructed efforts to mobilise NATO air forces against the Bosnian Serb forces.

Bratunac Brigade – The Bratunac Brigade was one of the three units, together with the Milići Infantry Brigade and the Skelani Independent Battalion, which together encircled Srebrenica. The soldiers of the Bratunac Brigade took part in mass shootings in Kravica and at

Branjevo Military Farm, as well as in the execution of detainees from the Cultural Centre in Pilica.

Crnogorac, Dragan – member of the Training Centre of the RS Police Jahorina Special Brigade. He pleaded guilty to crimes against humanity. The Court of Bosnia and Herzegovina sentenced him to 13 years' imprisonment.

10th Sabotage Detachment – the 10th Sabotage Detachment was a special unit of the General Staff, which was directly subordinated to the Intelligence Affairs Directorate headed by Colonel Petar Salapura, General Staff Intelligence Affairs Chief. It had a total of 50 to 60 persons organised in two platoons (in Vlasenica and in Bijeljina). This unit participated in fighting to secure the seizure of the city on 11th July 1995, and five days later its members executed around one thousand five hundred detainees from the Srebrenica enclave at Branjevo Agricultural Farm.

Drina Corps – was the last of six RS Army corps and was formed on 1st November 1992. The key reason for its establishment were pockets of free territory in Cerska, Srebrenica, Žepa, Goražde, and on the periphery of Višegrad, that the RS Army considered posed an increasing threat at the left bank of the Drina River. It was formed by combining and increasing the units of the existing East-Bosnia Corps and the Sarajevo-Romanija Corps. Together with the 10th Sabotage Detachment and the Special Police Brigade, the Drina Corps was a part of forces that ensured key resources and manpower for the genocide operation in Srebrenica.

Đurić, Mendeljejev – Commander of the First Company of the Jahorina Training Centre. The Court of Bosnia and Herzegovina found him guilty of genocide and sentenced him to 28 years' imprisonment.

Erdemović, Dražen – member of the 10th Sabotage Detachment. Pleaded guilty of crimes against humanity before the ICTY and was sentenced to five years' imprisonment.

Golijan, Vlastimir – member of the 10th Sabotage Detachment. The Court of Bosnia and Herzegovina found him guilty of crimes again humanity and sentenced him to 30 years' imprisonment.

Goronja, Zoran – member of the 10th Sabotage Detachment. Found guilty of crimes against humanity and sentenced to 15 years' imprisonment.

UN Dutch Battalion – the first Dutch units arrived in Srebrenica in February 1994. The so-called 'Dutchbat III' was the third Dutch unit in Srebrenica and arrived to the enclave in January 1995. Dutchbat III was actually the Thirteenth Air Mobile Battalion, a part of the Air Mobile Brigade of the Royal Netherlands Armed Forces. From the very beginning, from its arrival to the enclave and its deployment, the command of the Dutch Battalion refused to give up the stereotypes it had already adopted about the situation in Srebrenica. It treated the local population with condescension, while being obliging in their relations with the Serb forces, particularly Serb officers. Reports submitted from the enclave show that in July 1995, the Command of the Battalion either stood aside or, as in the case of the Battalion Deputy Commander Robert Franken, contributed to the covering up of the crimes.

Ivanović, Željko – Member of the Second Squad of Special Police Forces in Šekovići (RS MoI). The Court of Bosnia and Herzegovina found him guilty of genocide and sentenced him to 20 years' imprisonment.

Jević, Duško – Assistant Commander of the Special Police Brigade of RS MoI and Commander of the Special

Police Brigade Training Centre Jahorina. The Court of Bosnia and Herzegovina found him guilty of genocide and sentenced him to 32 years' imprisonment.

Jokić, Dragan – chief of engineering of the RS Army Zvornik Brigade. Sentenced before the ICTY for aiding and abetting extermination and persecution on political, racial and religious grounds (crimes against humanity) to nine years' imprisonment.

Karadžić, Radovan – one of the founders of the Serb Democratic Party (SDS) and its president until 19th July 1996 when he resigned; Chairman of the National Security Council of the so-called Serb Republic of Bosnia and Herzegovina, president of the three-member Presidency of RS from its establishment on 12th May 1992 to 17th December 1992, and thereafter the sole president of RS and Supreme Commander of its armed forces until July 1996. The first instance judgement found him guilty of genocide, persecution, extermination, murder, deportation, inhumane acts – forcible transfer, terror, unlawful attack on civilians and hostage-taking – and sentenced him to 40 years' imprisonment.

Karremans, Thomas (Thom/Ton) Jakob Peter – Commander of the Dutch Battalion in Srebrenica during the genocide operation in July 1995. The mandate of the Dutch Battalion was to protect the UN "safe zone" but the military and police forces of the RS/FRY seized it and killed over eight thousands boys and men in the course of five days. He was filmed while saluting Ratko Mladić, from whom he accepted gifts, and with whom he shook hands when departing from Srebrenica. During his testimony before the International Criminal Tribunal for the former Yugoslavia he said that when his request for aerial support was finally approved, it was "too little and too late".

Upon his return to the Netherlands following the fall of Srebrenica, he was promoted to Colonel and later retired.

Kojić, Stanko – member of the 10th Sabotage Detachment. He was found guilty before the Court of Bosnia and Herzegovina for crimes against humanity and sentenced to 32 years' imprisonment.

Kos, Franc – member of the 10th Sabotage Detachment. He was found guilty before the Court of Bosnia and Herzegovina for crimes against humanity, and sentenced to 35 years' imprisonment.

Krstić, Radislav – Chief of Staff and Deputy Commander of the Drina Corps of the RS Army. Appointed as the Drina Corps Commander on 13th July 1995. On 19th April 2004, the ICTY found him guilty for aiding and abetting genocide, crimes against humanity, and violation of the laws and customs of war, and sentenced him to 35 years' imprisonment.

Mothers of Srebrenica – survivors and victims of the genocide are organised in numerous associations, but there are three that stand out from the others. These are the associations who have gathered mothers, sisters, wives, and daughters of those slain, and are engaged in representing their interests. If it were not for them there would be no Memorial Centre, neither would it be located in Potočari, nor would it be a state institution. The "Movement of Mothers of Srebrenica and Žepa Enclaves" is an association with its seat in Sarajevo, "Women of Srebrenica" is located in Tuzla, while "Mothers of Srebrenica" works in Srebrenica.

The International Court of Justice in The Hague (ICJ) – is a legal body of the United Nations. The court's headquarters is in The Hague, Netherlands. It was established in 1945 by the United Nations Charter, and in 1993 it accepted, for the first time in its history, the case of violation of Convention on the Prevention and Punishment of the Crime of Genocide in the lawsuit of Bosnia and Herzegovina against the Federal Republic of Yugoslavia. The judgment in this case was pronounced in February 2007 and Serbia was found guilty of failing to prevent the genocide committed by the military and police forces of Bosnian Serbs.

International Criminal Tribunal for the former Yugoslavia (ICTY) – was established on 25th May 1993 by the United Nations Security Council Resolution 827 and is situated in The Hague. Officially, the Resolution was adopted in response to mass atrocities, ethnic cleansing and other serious violations of international humanitarian law committed in former Yugoslavia. The ICTY has charged 161 persons. Those indicted by the ICTY include heads of state, prime ministers, army chiefs-of-staff, interior ministers, and many other high- and mid-level political, military and police leaders from various parties to the Yugoslav conflicts. One of the most important achievements of the Hague Tribunal is the judicial establishment of facts on crimes committed in former Yugoslavia that are now irrefutable and incontestable. For the first time, the acts of rape committed by members of the Bosnian Serb armed forces were characterized as an instrument of terror. The Tribunal contributed to the personalisation of guilt for the crimes committed. The court established beyond doubt that the crimes committed against Muslims from Eastern Bosnia were crimes which would constitute genocide.

The Memorial Centre in Potočari – is located in the former battery factory in Potočari where the Dutch Battalion and its command were situated from 1994 to July 1995. It was established in May 2001 by decision of then High Representative for Bosnia and Herzegovina, Wolfgang

Petritsch, as a foundation with the aim of constructing and maintaining an architectural complex to honour the victims of genocide in Srebrenica in 1995. The first collective burial ceremony took place in 2003 when almost one thousand victims, 969 to be more precise, were buried in three phases: 600 victims in March, 282 in July, and 87 victims in September. The largest number of victims buried during one single ceremony was 775 in 2010. The remains of 7.033 genocide victims have so far been exhumed, out of which 6.930 have been finally or preliminary identified. 6.166 victims of genocide have been buried in the Potočari Memorial Centre, and another 230 victims in other cemeteries. The total number of buried victims is 6.396. In the coming years, the graves of almost a thousand victims who had been buried as incomplete skeletons will be exhumed in order for their subsequently discovered skeleton parts to be buried.

Miletić, Radivoje – Chief of Operations and Training of the Main Staff of the RS Army. Found guilty by the ICTY for crimes against humanity and sentenced to 18 years' imprisonment.

Milošević, Slobodan – President of the Republic of Serbia from 26th December 1990, President of the Federal Republic of Yugoslavia (FRY) from 15th July 1997 to 6th October 2000. As the FRY President he also was the President of the Supreme Council of FRY Defence and Supreme Commander of the Yugoslav Army. He died on 11th March 2006. The proceedings against him before the ICTY ended on 14th March 2006. He was indicted for genocide, complicity in genocide, deportation, murder, persecutions on political, racial or religious grounds, inhumane acts (forcible transfer), extermination, imprisonment, torture, wilful killing, unlawful confinement, wilfully causing great suffering, unlawful deportation or transfer, extensive destruction and appropriation of property, not justified by military necessity, cruel treatment, plunder of public or private property, attacks on civilians, destruction of or wilful damage to historic monuments and institutions dedicated to education or religion, unlawful attacks on civilian objects...

Mladić, Ratko – Colonel General, Chief Commander of the RS Army Main Staff. After 15 years of hiding from the international justice and the avoidance of legal prosecution, he was arrested in Serbia on 26th May 2011. The initial indictment against him was confirmed on 25th July 1995. He was charged with genocide, persecutions, extermination, murder, deportation, inhumane acts, violation of the laws or customs of war, terror, unlawful attacks on civilians, hostage taking. The trial commenced on 16th May 2012. The Prosecution was closed on 26th February 2014. The Defence case commenced on 19th May 2014. His trial is still in progress.

Morillon, Phillipe – the French General who commanded UNPROFOR forces in Bosnia and Herzegovina from 1992 to 1993. His engagement was instrumental in pronouncing Srebrenica a United Nations "safe zone". During his testimony before the Hague Tribunal, he presented the evidence on the participation of Serbian and Yugoslav units in attacks at Srebrenica in spring 1993. In September 2010, the families of victims of Srebrenica genocide prevented his visit to the Memorial Centre in Potočari.

Nikolić, Drago – 2nd Lieutenant and Chief of Security of the RS Army Zvornik Brigade. Found guilty by the ICTY of genocide and complicity to commit genocide, crimes against humanity and violations of the laws or customs of war. Sentenced to 35 years' imprisonment.

Nikolić, Momir – Assistant Commander for Security and Intelligence, Bratunac Brigade. In May 2003, he pleaded guilty of persecutions on political, racial, and religious grounds, and the ICTY Prosecution agreed to withdraw the remaining five counts of charges against Nikolić. Additionally, in the plea agreement, Nikolić agreed to testify in other proceedings before the Tribunal, including other trials related to Srebrenica. He was sentenced to 20 years' imprisonment.

Obrenović, Dragan – Chief of Staff and Deputy Commander of the Zvornik Infantry Brigade. He pleaded guilty of persecutions as crimes against humanity before the ICTY Prosecution in May 2003. He agreed to testify in other proceedings related to Srebrenica before the ICTY. He was sentenced to 17 years' imprisonment.

Pandurević, Vinko – Lieutenant-Colonel and Commander of the Zvornik Brigade of the RS Army Drina Corps. He was found guilty of crimes against humanity and violations of the laws or customs of war, and sentenced to 13 years' imprisonment.

The RS Police – The present Ministry of the Interior of the RS considers 4th April 1992 as the date of its establishment. During the aggression against RB&H, the RS MoI had units participating in combat, the Special Police Brigade, which was directly subordinate to the Minster's Cabinet, as well as special police units organised at regional level. While the Special Police Brigade was a separately formed unit, the special police units consisted of regular policemen who were organised in these special units for the needs and realisation of combat tasks. Special police units were part of centres of public security at regional level and were staffed with policemen from local police stations. During the war, the Special Police Brigade functioned as a combat unit. The Special Police Brigade Headquarters were in Janja. In July 1995, the Commander was Goran Sarić, and the Deputy Commander of the Special Police Brigade was Ljubomir Borovčanin. In the region of Podrinje, special police units were organised in the centre of public security located in Zvornik, headed by Dragomir Vasić. The Deputy Head of the Public Security Centre in Zvornik was Mane Đurić. Many high officials of the RS Police have already been convicted for their participation in different ways in the genocide operation following the fall of Srebrenica. Judgement by the International Court of Justice in The Hague found the RS police guilty of committing genocide against the Bosniak population of Eastern Bosnia.

Popović, Vujadin – Lieutenant Colonel and the Assistant Commander of Security of the staff of the Drina Corps of the RS Army. Found guilty of genocide, complicity to commit genocide, extermination, persecutions, murder, and sentenced to life imprisonment.

Srebrenica Genocide Memorial Room – a museum space located in the former headquarters of the UN Dutch Battalion in Potočari.

The Scorpions – a special antiterrorist unit of the Serbian Ministry of the Interior. The Scorpions unit was officially established by the oil industry of the so-called Republic of Serb Krajina in 1991 to secure oil fields in the area of Đeletovci and its surroundings. In 1993 the unit was renamed 'the Scorpions'. It first counted around 200 men and was under the command of the Vukovar Corps and General Dušan Lončar. During the following few years it took part in battles around Bihać and Velika Kladuša, as part of the armed forces under the control of Fikret Abdić. Later on they were sent to Trnovo, under the command of the Sarajevo-Romanija Corps and General Dragomir Milošević. In 1996, they were attached to the special antiterrorist unit of the Serbian Ministry of the Interior. In March 1999, the unit committed war crimes against the Albanian population in Podujevo. In June 2005, during the trial of Slobodan Milošević, the Tribunal in the Hague played a video showing members of the Serbian special police forces unit, the Scorpions, executing six Bosniaks near Trnovo in July 1995.

Trbić, Milorad – assistant to Drago Nikolić, Chief of Security of Drina Corps Zvornik Brigade to whom he directly reported. Sentenced to 20 years' imprisonment before the Court of Bosnia and Herzegovina.

RS/FRY Army – established on 12th May 1992 when Ratko Mladić was named as its Commander at the so-called Assembly of Serb people in Bosnia and Herzegovina. It was created from the arms, logistics, staff, and organisational structure of the Yugoslav National Army. The 30th Personnel Centre of the Yugoslav Army Main Staff was in charge of military and logistic support to the RS Army. The Yugoslav Army paid salaries and managed other status issues of RS Army officers and soldiers through this centre. Almost the entire RS Army Main Staff was indicted or convicted by the ICTY for crimes committed in Bosnia and Herzegovina, as well as a significant part of the Yugoslav Army Main Staff including two chiefs: Momčilo Perišić and Dragoljub Ojdanić. The RS Army is the first armed formation found guilty for the crime of genocide before the International Court of Justice in The Hague. The Court explicitly stated that genocide against Muslims in Bosnia and Herzegovina was executed by the Army and the Ministry of the Interior of RS. According to the judgment of the International Court of Justice in The

Hague, the RS Army was found guilty of committing genocide against the Bosniak population of Eastern Bosnia.

Vuković, Radomir – member of the 2nd Squad of the RS Ministry of the Interior Special Police in Šekovići. Found guilty of genocide and sentenced to 20 years' imprisonment by the Court of Bosnia and Herzegovina.

Zvornik Infantry Brigade – formed on 2nd June 1992, in the so-called Serb Municipality of Zvornik. Three large-scale executions between 14th and 16th July were committed in the zone of responsibility of the Zvornik Brigade, and its Commander, Chief-of-Staff, Assistant Commander for Security and Assistant Commander for Engineering have been convicted of complicity to commit genocide and crimes against humanity.

CHRONOLOGY

9th January, 1992 – establishment of the so-called Serb Republic of Bosnia and Herzegovina, which was later named Republika Srpska (RS).

April 1992 – units of YNA Novi Sad Corps and paramilitary forces occupied the town of Srebrenica without resistance;

12th May, 1992 – the so-called Assembly of the Serb Republic of Bosnia and Herzegovina decided on six strategic goals of the Serb People in Bosnia and Herzegovina;

19th May, 1992 – Serb forces withdraw from Srebrenica under pressure from the Territorial Defence of Bosnia and Herzegovina;

November 1992 – "Directive 4" by General Ratko Mladić to the Drina Corps; orders to forcibly displace the Muslim population of Podrinje: "if there is no consent – respond with destruction";

May 1992 – April 1993 – life becomes unbearably cruel in the enclave; the siege of Srebrenica by Bosnian Serb forces and regular YNA units, later the Yugoslav Army;

January 1993 – American president Bill Clinton decides to airdrop food to the enclaves in Eastern Bosnia;

16th April, 1993 – "Safe Area Srebrenica"; the UN Security Council adopts Resolution 819 which formally declares the "UN safe zones" of Srebrenica and Žepa;

18th April, 1993 – Ceasefire Agreement between the RB&H Army and the RS Army. Disarmament of RB&H Army forces begins in Srebrenica;

April 1993 – UNHCR's evacuations commence; due to the extremely difficult humanitarian situation, UNHCR evacuated eight to nine thousand people from Srebrenica;

July 1994 – RS Army Main Staff suspended the Ceasefire Agreement from 18th April 1993; the Drina Corps received orders to reduce the UN protected zones to the territory of the town – in case of Srebrenica, and a territory of three kilometres – in the case of Žepa;

Spring 1995 – Radovan Karadžić issues "Directive 7" of the Supreme Command; the Drina Corps receives orders to "create an unbearable situation of total insecurity, with no hope of further survival or life for the inhabitants of Srebrenica or Žepa through planned and well-thought-out everyday combat operations";

Spring 1995 – Naser Orić, Commander of the 28th Division of the RB&H Army, leaves Srebrenica;

3rd June, 1995 – following the orders by the Drina Corps Commander, units of the Bratunac Brigade and mobile combat group "Wolves of the Drina" took over the UN post in Zeleni Jadar;

28th June, 1995 – on the Serb religious holiday of St. Vitus, Radovan Karadžić and Momčilo Krajišnik make the "Krivaja-95" plan public;

2nd July, 1995 – RS Army Drina Corps C issues the "Orders to go into offensive action" and directs the beginning of realisation of the operation "Krivaja-95";

6th July, 1995 – Serb forces bomb the city from the early morning;

8th July, 1995 – armed skirmishes are intensified;

10th July, 1995 – Commander of UN forces in Srebrenica promises aerial attacks to protect the enclave;

11th July, 1995 (around 4:00 p.m.) – RS Army forces enter Srebrenica; civilian and armed men form a line and start moving towards Tuzla;

12th July, 1995 (around 2:00 p.m.) – deportation of the civilian population from Potočari begins; men are kept in the "White House" across from the UN Dutch Base;

13th July, 1995 – in the early evening, members of the RS Army and Ministry of the Interior execute over a thousand detainees in the warehouse of the Agricultural Co-operative in Kravica;

14th July, 1995 – during the early morning hours the transportation of detainees from Bratunac to Zvornik begins; in the afternoon, the mass execution in Orahovac starts;

15th July, 1995 – shooting in Petkovci; continuation of transfer of detainees; execution in Pilica continues;

16th July, 1995 – members of the 10th Sabotage Detachment shoot around 1,500 prisoners at the Military Agricultural Farm Branjevo; on the same day over five hundred detainees are killed in the Cultural Centre in Pilica;

21st July, 1995 – Dutch Battalion leaves Srebrenica;

27th September – 2nd October, 1995 – Operation "Sanitation"; excavation of primary mass graves, transfer of bodies and concealment of actions.

SREBRENICA
MCMXCV

SREBRENICA
MCMXCV

_____

_____

_____

_____

_____

_____

_____

_____

_____

_____

_____

_____

_____

_____

_____

_____

_____

_____

_____

_____

_____

_____

SREBRENICA
MCMXCV

SREBRENICA
MCMXCV

Following the capture of Srebrenica by the military and police forces of the Republika Srpska on 11th July 1995, the long
-term strategy of elimination of
Bosniaks from Eastern Bosnia
reached a new stage of realisation. The extermination of Bosnian Muslims began with several
years of torture within the enclave of Srebrenica, followed by
the operation of forced displacement of the women and children,
and then by the systematic execution of boys and men of every
age. The International Court of
Justice in The Hague (ICJ) and
the International Criminal Tribunal for the former Yugoslavia
(ICTY) ruled that these crimes,
carried out by the army and police forces of the Republika Srpska, were acts of genocide.